LEADERSHIP:
HOW TO LEAD,
HOW TO LIVE

By D. QUINN MILLS

HARVARD BUSINESS SCHOOL

©Copyright 2005 by D. Quinn Mills

Revised Edition, 2006.

All rights reserved. No part of this work may be reproduced, stored in a retrieval system, or transcribed in any form or by any means (electronic, mechanical, photocopying, recording or otherwise) without the prior written permission of the publisher, MindEdge Press, 1601 Trapelo Road, Waltham, MA 02451.

MindEdge Press
1601 Trapelo Road
Waltham, MA 02451

www.mindedge.com

Printed in the United States

CONTENTS

PART I. BEING A LEADER

Chapter 1. The Importance of Leadership

Chapter 2. Learning to Be a Leader

Chapter 3. Finding Our Basis for Leadership

PART II. THE CENTRAL ELEMENTS OF LEADERSHIP

Chapter 4. Being a Successful Leader

Chapter 5. Leading at the Office

Chapter 6. Partnering with Others in Leadership

PART III. BUILDING OUR CAREERS TO LEADERSHIP POSITIONS

Chapter 7. Career Paths to Leadership

Chapter 8. Starting Our Careers

Chapter 9. Advancing Along the Path to Leadership

Chapter 10. Career Hurdles We Create

Chapter 11. Leading a Team

Chapter 12. Leadership in the Midst of External Change

PART IV. THE PLACE OF LEADERSHIP IN OUR LIVES

Chapter 13. Sustaining Leadership via a Balanced Life

Chapter 14. Leadership and Personal Fulfillment

PART I

BEING A LEADER

PREFACE

Leadership: How to Lead, How to Live is written to help working professionals better understand the principles and methods of leadership and how leadership affects our lives. This book shares years of experience and expertise in a readily accessible framework.

Leadership: How to Lead, How to Live is in four parts, designed to properly introduce leadership:

PART I. BEING A LEADER

PART II. THE CENTRAL ELEMENTS OF LEADERSHIP

PART III. BUILDING OUR CAREERS TO A LEADERSHIP POSITION

PART IV. THE PLACE OF LEADERSHIP IN OUR LIVES

Part I

The Purpose of This Book

This book's primary purpose is to help each of us understand leadership. We all spend much of our lives being responsive to leaders—business, social, and political leaders—so it is useful and important to better understand the sources, strengths, and limitations of those who seek to be our leaders.

Another purpose of this book is to enable those of us who wish to do so to begin to develop ourselves as leaders, and to embark on a path of personal development that will continue throughout our lifetimes. Learning to be a leader also requires practice—trying to exert leadership with other people—and that we must do on our own.

The objectives of this book are:

- To convey the key characteristics of leadership.

- To show you how to be a leader.

- To help you clarify your own principles and understand how these principles will guide you as a leader.

- To give you a deeper comprehension of your own values, and to help you recognize how you will respond under pressure if your values are challenged.

This book is organized into four parts. Part 1 is about becoming a leader, what leadership is and how to learn the role. Part 2 is about how to be an effective leader. Part 3 is about how to develop your career into a position of leadership. Part 4 is about how to lead a life that is balanced between

Leadership: How to Lead, How to Live

work and family, so that you can become a more effective leader and be the person you want to be at the same time.

Chapter 1

The Importance of Leadership

Management is doing things right; leadership is doing the right things.

- Peter F. Drucker, management thinker

Few things are more important to human activity than leadership. Effective leadership helps our nation through times of peril. It makes a business organization successful. It enables a not-for-profit organization to fulfill its mission. The effective leadership of parents enables children to grow strong and healthy and become productive adults.

The absence of leadership is equally dramatic in its effects. Without leadership, organizations move too slowly, stagnate, and lose their way. Much of the literature about organizations stresses decision-making and implies that if decision-making is timely, complete, and correct, then things will go well. Yet a decision by itself changes nothing. After a decision is made, an organization faces the problem of implementation—how to get things done in a timely and effective way.

Problems of implementation are really issues about how leaders influence behavior, change the course of events, and overcome resistance. Leadership is crucial in implementing decisions successfully.

Each of us recognizes the importance of leadership when we vote for our political leaders. We realize that it matters who is in office, so we participate in a contest, an election, to choose the best candidate.

Investors recognize the importance of business leadership when they say that a good leader can make a success of a weak business plan, but that a poor leader can ruin even the best plan.

Who Will Gain from Leadership?

Do you want to be a leader? Or, if you're already a leader, do you want to improve your leadership? Do you want to affect what other people do—to help them accomplish important goals? Do you want to point the way in your organization? Do you want to climb the promotion ladder to positions of higher authority and greater pay? Leadership will make these things possible.

You should read this book if:

- You are interested in leadership and how it affects you.
- You plan to lead an organization or are already in a leadership position.
- You are interested in developing yourself to meet the challenges you will confront in a leadership role.
- You wish to make a difference in the world through leadership.

The Meaning of Leadership

What is leadership? It is a process by which one person influences the thoughts, attitudes, and behaviors of others. Leaders set a direction for the rest of us; they help us see what lies ahead; they help us visualize what we might achieve; they encourage us and inspire us. Without leadership a group of human beings quickly degenerates into argument and conflict, because we see things in different ways and lean toward different solutions. Leadership helps to point us in the same direction and harness our efforts jointly. Leadership is the ability to get other people to do something significant that they might not otherwise do. It's energizing people toward a goal.

Without followers, however, a leader isn't a leader, although followers may only come after a long wait. For example, during the 1930s Winston Churchill urged his fellow Englishmen to face the coming threat from Hitler's Germany. But most Englishmen preferred to believe that Hitler could be appeased—so that a war could be avoided. They were engaged in wishful thinking about the future and denial that the future would be dangerous. They resented Churchill for insisting that they must face the danger. They rejected his leadership. He had very few followers. But finally reality intruded—Germany went too far and war began. At this point Churchill was acclaimed for his foresight, and became prime minister of the United Kingdom during the Second World War. During this period almost all Englishmen accepted his leadership willingly.

True leadership is sometimes hard to distinguish from false leadership, which is merely a form of pretending. Winston Churchill was a real and great leader. But there are also people who wish to appear to be leaders, but aren't actually. They say that they are leading others; they posture as if they are setting direction and inspiring others. Yet often they are merely pretending. There's an old saying that the way to become a leader is to find a parade and run to the front of it. We refer to a person "leading" a parade, but walking at the front isn't really leadership unless the person in front is actually choosing the direction! If the person isn't choosing the direction, then being at the front of the line is merely a way to pretend to be a leader.

Leadership can be used for good or ill. Hitler seemed to be a leader of the German people, but he set an evil direction. He had great leadership skills, but put them to terrible uses. Sometimes people in business use leadership skills to exploit others. Sometimes people in charitable organizations use leadership skills to benefit themselves rather than the people they are supposed to help. Leadership skills can be perverted to pursue bad ends.

The Importance of Ethics

The danger that leadership will be perverted is why ethics are so important to good leadership. Ethics are the inner compass that directs a person toward what is right and fair. Only if a person has an inner ethical compass can he or she be sure that leadership qualities will not turn to evil ends.

Learning to lead with good objectives is the only purpose of this book. So let us say that those who do harm are not leaders at all; we recognize that they may be influential and persuasive, but we will not think of them as leaders.

With confidence that you, good readers of this book, will put leadership to noble ends, we go forward.

The Work of the Leader

Taking a leadership position means several things: A leader must have a vision of the future for the organization and its members.

EXECUTIVE SUMMARY 1-1

TAKING A LEADERSHIP POSITION

Taking a leadership position means:

- Having a vision about what can be accomplished.

- Making a commitment to the mission and to the people you lead.

- Taking responsibility for the accomplishment of the mission and the welfare of those you lead.

- Assuming risk of loss and failure.

- Accepting recognition for success.

A leader must be able to express his or her vision clearly and in a compelling manner so that others are engaged by it. (See Executive Summary 1-1.)

A leader has to make a commitment to his or her vision, to the organization, and to the members of the organization. A leader can't be committed one day and uninterested the next. People will judge a leader by his or her commitment, and will commit themselves no more than the leader does.

A leader assumes a considerable amount of responsibility—not just for the mission that he or she urges others to accept, nor just for the organization he or she heads, but for his or her followers, their lives and efforts, as well.

The Importance of Leadership

A leader assumes risk. If there is no risk, little leadership is required. If the effort is easy and certain to succeed, anyone can, and probably will, "lead" it. But where the effort entails a risk of failure, then many people will quail before the challenge and leadership is necessary to get people to make the commitment and the effort to succeed.

In most organizations, one associates high levels of leadership with high levels of authority. The chief executive of a company usually plays more of a leadership role than people at lower levels of the hierarchy in the firm. It is the same in not-for-profits and government agencies. The higher on the job ladder a person is, the more she is expected to exhibit leadership.

In the military, however, the opposite holds true, and for a very good reason. In the military the greatest leadership challenge is to get other people to risk their lives in combat. Generally, the higher one goes in the chain of command, the less exposure he has to the battlefield, and the less exposure to men and women who are in combat.

The officers who have responsibility for commanding soldiers in combat have the greatest leadership challenge, for they must get others to risk their lives. Michael Jordan's brother is an army sergeant major leading a deployment in Iraq in which he is responsible for more than 2,000 soldiers. Offered an opportunity to leave his assignment in combat, he chose to stay with his unit in harm's way. In so doing, he accepted one of the military's most significant leadership challenges.

The first responsibility in a position of leadership is to have a vision. (See Executive Summary 1-2.) The visionary leader must create his or her concept of what the organization can accomplish. A business leader may be leading a few people in a department or an entire company; a military leader a small squad or an entire army. The vision may be smaller when the group of people is small; and much broader when the group of people is large, but it must be forward-looking and exciting in either case.

EXECUTIVE SUMMARY 1-2

VISIONARY LEADERSHIP

Visionary leadership requires:

- Creating a vision, a mission, and a strategy.

- Communicating the vision/mission/strategy and getting buy-in.

- Motivating action.

- Helping an organization grow, evolve, and adapt to changing circumstances.

---❖---

The leader must also provide a mission—what needs to be done—and a strategy, a path, for how to accomplish the mission and achieve the vision, a way for the group to get there. But having an exciting vision, an exciting mission, and a careful strategy is not sufficient. A leader must clearly communicate them. Only if people grasp the vision can they commit to it, and buy-in is crucial to motivating action. Finally, a vision cannot be rigid and unchanging; it must adapt to changing circumstances, growing and evolving. Otherwise it becomes outdated and obsolete, and loses its power to excite and motivate people.

Leaders versus Administrators and Managers

Leadership is not the same thing as being in a position of authority. It is possible to be a boss in a company without being a leader. A boss can be more of an administrator than a leader.

Conversely, an administrator can be effective in his job without being a leader. The administrator is a bureaucrat—whether in government or in business—a person who keeps careful records and sees that things are done according to the rules. On the other hand, a leader can be effective without being an administrator—leaving rules, regulations, and their enforcement to others.

Administration is not as exciting a topic as leadership, but it is almost as important. The success of organizations depends to a great degree on how well they are administered. A manager is often thought to be primarily an administrator. But a manager is not an administrator; management requires a special set of skills of its own. And being a manager is different from being a leader, as we shall see below. So there are three roles: administrator, manager, and leader.

A manager has the broadest role, and a good manager has much of an administrator and a leader in him or her. A manager needs to set direction and inspire others to get work done (leadership functions) and to keep records and see that rules are followed (administrative functions).

The manager is a necessary combination of leader and administrator. (See D. Quinn Mills, **Principles of Management**, Waltham, MA: MindEdge Press, 2005.) But leadership is the most important of the three roles.

Administrators

What does an administrator do? (See Executive Summary 1-3.) An administrator applies rules and regulations generally developed by top executives of an organization. (In the government, the key rules and regulations are often issued by legislative authorities like the U.S. Congress). He or she keeps records and fills out forms necessary to take administrative steps (like getting employees paid or reimbursing an employee for travel expenses).

EXECUTIVE SUMMARY 1-3

ELEMENTS OF ADMINISTRATION

The elements of administration are:

- Making rules and regulations

- Making decisions that apply and interpret rules and regulations

- Keeping records

- Filling out forms

Managers

What does a manager do? (See Executive Summary 1-4.) He or she makes plans and creates budgets that set forth in great detail how something will be accomplished and how much money and other resources (e.g., people, office space) are necessary to accomplish those plans and budgets. He decides who is going to be assigned to the necessary tasks and how they will fit into the organization. She supervises the actions people take, ensuring that they are doing the right things, that no money is being misappropriated or wasted (we call this "controlling"), and when problems arise she helps to resolve them. Finally, by combining these tasks into a coherent whole, the manager makes the organization operate efficiently.

Running an organization effectively requires administration, management, and leadership. Leadership is ordinarily in shorter supply than administrative or managerial competence. Leadership is more important and more demanding for most people. Fewer people are able or willing to be leaders, so it tends to be a higher calling than administration or management.

There is a large literature discussing the differences between leaders and managers. There is also an important distinction to make between leaders and administrators. In general, a leader takes a broader view and points an organization toward necessary, even critical, change.

The core of the criticism in the literature is that organizations of all sorts (corporations, government agencies, and not-for-profit organizations) tend to be over-managed (and/or over-administrated) and under-led. Because of over-management and over-administration, organizations are slow to make necessary changes and achieve less than what they could. This is a substantial criticism that points to the importance of leadership.

EXECUTIVE SUMMARY 1-4

ELEMENTS OF MANAGEMENT

The elements of management are:

- Planning and budgeting
- Setting direction
- Organizing and staffing
- Aligning the efforts of many people
- Controlling
- Decision-making and problem solving
- Motivating and inspiring people

The Nature of Leadership

True leadership is special, subtle, and complex. Too often we confuse things like personal style and a position of authority with leadership.

- Leadership is not primarily a particular personality trait. A trait closely linked to leadership is charisma, but many people who have charisma (for example, movie actors and sports figures) are not leaders.

- Leadership is not primarily a set of important objectives. It involves getting things done.

- Leadership is not primarily a formal position. There have been great leaders who did not hold high positions—for example, Martin Luther King, Jr. and Jeanne d'Arc—and there are people who hold high positions who are not leaders at all, but administrators who don't want to rock the boat.

- Leadership is not primarily a set of behaviors. Many leadership manuals suggest that what defines leadership is things such as delegating and providing inspiration and vision; but people who are not leaders can do these things, and some effective leaders don't do them all.

Many discussions of leadership confuse any and all of the above—personality, important objectives, formal position, specific behaviors—with leadership. (See John P. Kotter, **What Leaders Really Do**, Boston: Harvard Business School Press, 1999.) But leadership is more than any of the above characteristics. Leadership is a process by which one influences the thoughts and behaviors of others in a substantial way. It may involve charisma, important objectives, a formal position, and a particular set of behaviors, but it is not limited to any of them.

Effective leaders are often very complex people. Writing about Oliver Cromwell, the Lord Protector of England during the English civil wars of the seventeenth century, a foremost historian marveled at the complexity of his personality. "There was no single Cromwell," he wrote, "—that is, a clear-cut individual...Instead, there was a multiplicity of Cromwells, each linked to the other by his enormous vitality...Firstly, there was the very human, simple and compassionate man, a visionary and a romantic. Secondly, there was a violent, boisterous and irascible bully. Thirdly, there was the resolute and iron-willed general...Fourthly, the calculating politician, the man of expedients who had no guiding principles. And lastly, there was…the Cromwell…who, as the interpreter of God's will, was capable of committing any atrocity." (J. F. C. Fuller, **A Military History of the Western World**, Volume 2, New York: Funk & Wagnalls, 1955, p. 110.)

Because leaders can be so complex, we must be careful in our generalizations about leaders and their personalities. We must consider the individuality of each leader. But not all leaders are such complex personalities, which is good for most of us who aspire to leadership.

Examples of Leadership

Leadership in Business

In the 1980s Harley-Davidson was almost knocked out of business by competition from other firms. To survive, it needed to change dramatically. Rich Teerlink, the company's leader, was able to save the firm financially, but with the pressure off, the challenge of continuing to improve seemed even more daunting.

Could Teerlink get his managers and employees to make the significant, and to many of them inconvenient, changes necessary?

He did it by building a different company, one driven from the bottom up rather than from the top down by managers. It's a story of successes and failures, advances and setbacks, dead ends and breakthroughs, ending in a much stronger company than before. (Read the inspiring story in Rich Teerlink and Lee Ozley, **More Than a Motorcycle: The Leadership Journey at Harley-Davidson**, Boston: Harvard Business School Press, 2000.)

Leadership in Government

When Charles O. Rossotti became commissioner of the Internal Revenue Service (IRS) in 1997, the agency had the largest customer base—and the lowest approval rating—of any institution in America. Mired in scandal, caught in a political maelstrom, and beset by profound management and technology problems, the IRS was widely dismissed as a hopelessly flawed and dysfunctional organization. Rossotti—the first businessperson to head the IRS—transformed the much-maligned agency.

In the glare of intense public scrutiny, he effected dramatic changes in the way the IRS did business—while the agency continued to collect $2 trillion in revenue. Through heated congressional hearings, encounters with Washington bigwigs, frank exchanges with taxpayers and employees, and risky turnaround strategies, Rossotti demonstrated leadership against daunting odds. (Read this enlightening story in Charles O. Rossotti, **Many Unhappy Returns: One Man's Quest to Turn Around the Most Unpopular Organization in America**, Boston: Harvard Business School Press, 2005.)

Leadership: How to Lead, How to Live

CHAPTER REFERENCES:

Fuller, J. F. C. **A Military History of the Western World.** Volume 2. New York: Funk and Wagnalls, 1955.

Kotter, John P. **What Leaders Really Do.** Boston: Harvard Business School Press, 1999

Mills, D. Quinn. **Principles of Management.** Waltham, MA: MindEdge Press, 2005.

Rossotti, Charles O. **Many Unhappy Returns: One Man's Quest to Turn Around the Most Unpopular Organization in America.** Boston: Harvard Business School Press, 2005.

Teerlink, Richard and Lee Ozley. **More Than a Motorcycle: The Leadership Journey at Harley-Davidson.** Boston: Harvard Business School Press, 2000.

ADDITIONAL READINGS:

Armstrong, Lance. **It's Not About the Bike: My Journey Back to Life.** New York: G.P. Putnam's Sons, 2000.

Bennis, Warren. **On Becoming a Leader.** Cambridge, MA: Perseus Books, 2003.

Gandossy, Robert and Jeffrey Sonnenfeld, editors. **Leadership and Governance from the Inside Out.** Hoboken, N.J.: John Wiley & Sons, 2004.

Leadership: How to Lead, How to Live

Chapter 2

Learning to Be a Leader

The most dangerous leadership myth is that leaders are born, that there is a genetic factor to leadership. This myth asserts that people simply either have certain charismatic qualities or not. That's nonsense; in fact, the opposite is true. Leaders are made rather than born.

- Warren Bennis, management thinker

Leadership: How to Lead, How to Live

In the first chapter we saw how important leadership is and we identified both what it is, and what it is not. In this chapter we see that each of us can become a leader, if we want to enough, and that there are a number of ways leadership emerges. Finally, we will consider some of the obstacles to leadership and how to overcome them.

Leadership: Innate, Bestowed, or Learned

Many people think leadership is innate. They believe its only source is natural charisma—a term that connotes charm, a winning personality, appeal, and allure. They believe that a good leader *must* possess charisma of some kind and that he or she knows when and how to apply the personal magnetism that is the essence of charisma. Charisma is so tied up with leadership in the minds of many people that we have to include it as both a basis for leadership and a quality of leaders.

Charisma is a subtle and complex quality that takes different forms in different human societies. It is not the same thing in America as it is in East Asia; nor the same as it is in the Muslim world. In America charisma is a combination of appearance, style, focus, confidence, and drive. Charismatic people have great influence on others. They have the capability to energize, inspire, and encourage people to be and act their best. If a leader is not charismatic, then no matter how intelligent he is or what a wonderful administrator he is, he will not be able to inspire his organization to follow him and execute his vision, and therefore he will never be an effective leader.

On the other hand, even if a leader is not the best administrator, or even if she is not the most clever person, if she is charismatic, then she will be able to recruit outstanding people to follow her, and she'll inspire them to perform at the highest level of their ability. Charisma also enables a leader to better interact with and influence the wide variety of people who have an impact on his or her organization, including shareholders, creditors, analysts, journalists, and political figures.

As noted earlier, some people have a natural charisma; but for other aspiring leaders it is the most difficult quality to acquire. Many people think that a person must have an attractive or alluring personality in order to become a leader.

The way in which a charismatic leader inspires others, instills vision and energizes collective action is a unique and valuable skill that should not be undervalued because it seems to lack a logical foundation. To many people, logic and rationality are boring. To them, leadership without natural charismatic spunk means a lack of the spirit of challenge, the desire to accomplish the impossible, to push to extremes of commitment and performance, and reach for goals that change the shape of our lives. In such a view, there is nothing motivating about always taking the safe, rational road. Charismatic leaders are the fuel of inspiration, change, and revolution. Criticism of charismatic leadership may in fact be directed at unquestioning, mindless following.

It is true, of course, that people with natural charisma are more readily accepted by others as leaders; but it is not crucial to possess natural charisma to become a leader. There are numerous examples throughout history of people who were not naturally charismatic yet became great leaders. Indeed, there are numerous examples of people today who lack innate charisma but have become effective leaders. We'll see some examples below.

It is also true that people look for leadership in those who occupy positions of authority. Many believe that leadership is bestowed—that it comes with a position of authority.

But a person can be in a position of authority without being an effective leader. Those of us who've worked in large organizations (corporate, governmental, or not-for-profit) often have seen people in high positions—positions of authority—who do not fit our definition of leadership. They are primarily administrators but not leaders. How do they reach the top of organizations without being leaders?

There are several ways. They may be promoted by seniority into positions that require leadership skills, although they lack them. They may use political skills and cunning to reach high positions in which their lack of leadership skills becomes unfortunately apparent. They may be able to exercise leadership at lower-level positions, but become paralyzed by the greater responsibilities at higher levels and retreat into administrative behavior.

It follows that leadership is not limited to the naturally charismatic, nor is it limited to those who are selected for a position of authority. Furthermore, people who have charisma are not always leaders, as we've seen; and those who have high positions aren't always leaders either.

What should the standard be by which leaders influence others? To me, rational argument and a sound decision-making process provide a better, more sustainable basis than a leader's persuasiveness. If followers understand a leader's rationale and that process was fair and sound, buy-in becomes easier to achieve. In addition, the former is less susceptible to the personal objectives and biases of both the leader and the follower.

Yet, the reality is that most positions of power involve some kind of election or interview process where the candidate who presents himself or herself the best (possibly a form of charisma) has a leg up on the other candidates. The bigger the role the more elaborate the selection process, and the more charisma plays a part. Charisma, seen in this perspective, is simply a function of the way our corporate/political landscape operates today.

Can those of us without natural charisma become leaders? Can those of us who are not yet in high positions of authority exercise leadership? The answer to both questions is yes.

EXECUTIVE SUMMARY 2-1

HOW LEADERS EMERGE

Leadership emerges in some people because they:

- Seem to have it naturally—it is innate.

- Are expected to show it in their jobs—it is bestowed on them.

- Have learned how to be effective leaders.

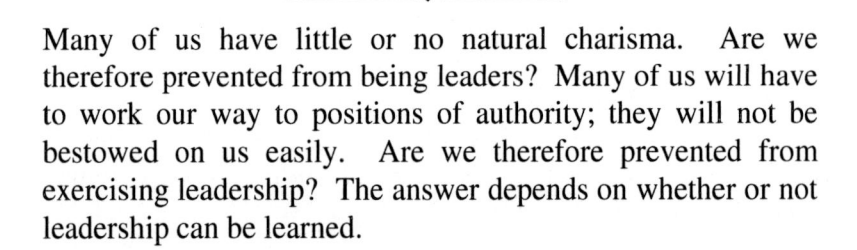

---❖---

Many of us have little or no natural charisma. Are we therefore prevented from being leaders? Many of us will have to work our way to positions of authority; they will not be bestowed on us easily. Are we therefore prevented from exercising leadership? The answer depends on whether or not leadership can be learned.

Later in this book (in Part 3) we will examine how leadership and career progress can combine to take a person to positions of authority in which the scope for his or her leadership is greatly enlarged. For the moment, however, we want to investigate the interaction between natural charisma and effective leadership.

Leadership usually requires us to interact to some substantial degree with others. We may have to speak at large gatherings, meet with people we haven't previously known and yet persuade them on a course of action, and huddle frequently with people who work for us. Leadership is rarely exercised in privacy. It is almost always an interpersonal matter.

Some of us are extroverts who find the interpersonal aspect of leadership engaging. Others are introverts, who find the interpersonal aspect of leadership daunting. Some of us lie in the middle of the psychological spectrum, a little extroverted and a little introverted. We aren't sure how we feel about undertaking leadership ourselves.

It would be unfortunate to let the lack of having an extroverted personality serve as a major barrier to our becoming leaders. It would limit our career options and deprive our communities and companies of much that we have to offer.

Can We Learn to be Leaders?

What if we are never able to become quite psychologically comfortable with the interpersonal aspect of leadership? Can I learn to put on a display of confidence that impresses people with my leadership ability? If I do so, am I acting? Is acting like a leader when I don't really feel comfortable dealing with others unethical? Shouldn't people accept me for what I am rather than what I pretend to be? Shouldn't others recognize the leader who is concealed beneath my shy exterior?

If I do act the extrovert, does it mean that I'm not a real leader, but only pretending? Will others sense artificiality in me, to the extent that I lose my credibility with them? Isn't it true, or shouldn't it be true, that real leadership exists when one is strong enough to reveal chinks in his or her armor honestly—

because after all, we are all human? Isn't leadership something we should strive toward naturally and honestly?

Admirable as such sentiments are, they may be unduly idealistic. Because of the importance of personal interactions in leadership (see Chapter 3), some business leaders define leadership as primarily the ability to energize others. But to argue that a leader must be naturally and honestly extroverted is rather limiting. Many of us are not naturally extroverted; in fact, many top political and business leaders are not "naturals" at all, but instead have learned to lead as if they are playing one of the most important roles in life.

Leadership as a Role in Life

It's helpful to think of the role of leadership as a mission, rather than as acting or pretending. Like some other important roles in life, we can choose or reject it, just as we can choose or reject being a spouse or parent. Each of us can decide to accept the role of leader, and achieve it if we make the necessary effort. Deciding to be a leader may come with personal costs, risks, and sacrifices. Real leadership is not a romantic exercise in ego satisfaction, but a choice we should make soberly and with recognition of what it may entail. But it is something almost any of us can decide to pursue.

When we think of leadership as a role, we must be careful not to lose sight of the importance of honesty, character, and personal commitment and not to infer that there is a successful recipe for being a good leader. If one approaches leadership in a formulaic way, then others will sense artificiality and not be inclined to follow. If one sees leadership as a role to play merely in the acting or pretending sense, then he or she will not inspire others to follow because they are very likely to see through the act.

Learning to Be a Leader

Evidence suggests that for many successful leaders, leadership is a role they have learned. Certainly for some people leadership comes naturally; but others can learn it; and still others overcome handicaps to display it. Many of the most effective leaders in business and public life have been introverts.

President George W. Bush, for example, appeared to people who knew him as a boy and a young man to be very shy; he has had to master reticence to be a leader. Václav Havel, the first president of the Czech Republic after it emerged in the early 1990s from Communist domination, was a quiet writer who never imagined that he would become a political leader.

Each of us has weaknesses; part of being able to lead is finding ways to overcome those weaknesses. Most of us have insecurities, and it takes a lot of effort and resolve to overcome them. It is okay for an emerging leader to have weaknesses as long as he or she recognizes and works hard to overcome them.

What does it mean to say that leadership is a role? It doesn't mean that all leaders are actors, pretending to be someone else as movie actors do. It's possible to play a role without pretending. For example, in a family, both parents have roles to play, but ordinarily they are not pretending in their roles. Similarly, a leader is playing a role, but not pretending. In playing a role, the leader is fulfilling expectations that other people have of him or her. In the case of leaders, that expectation is for what we call leadership.

Octavian was a nephew of Julius Caesar; he ultimately became the first emperor of Rome. He took the title Augustus and established the empire's first dynasty. He put an end to decades of civil war and expanded the empire to nearly its greatest size. He was a great leader.

What did he think of his leadership? On his deathbed he said to his family, "If I have played my role well, then dismiss me from the stage with applause." Here was one of history's outstanding leaders explicitly describing his leadership as a role.

It is important to recognize that people respond to the role, not to the person; just as they respond in a movie theater to the role an actor is playing rather than to the actor behind the role. Thus, when we act like leaders, other people often accept us in that role. It's the role one is playing to which others respond, not to oneself as an individual. This is why leaders come in so many different shapes, sizes, and ages.

Consider this: We each play several roles in our own lives (child, parent, breadwinner, ballplayer, musical performer), and we do so effectively. We can then add leadership to our list of roles.

It is useful to think of leadership as a role even for those who come naturally to leadership. Even a natural leader must be aware that she or he is "leading." Thinking of leadership as a role you are filling makes you recognize that you have a responsibility to the people you are leading. This is very important. Many people who have exercised leadership for the wrong purposes did so because they did not recognize their responsibility to those they were leading, but saw leadership only as a personal matter—as, if you will, an ego trip.

It is also useful to think of leadership as a role because it enables one to reach for a higher level of performance as a leader. If I am a leader but want to become a better leader, I can mentally put myself out of my comfort zone by playing the role of the better leader in order to improve myself.

A secretary of state of the United States visited with friends one night in a hotel room before giving a speech to a large audience. In that room, among people he'd known for many years, he was relaxed, joking—one of the guys. Then an aide to the secretary stuck his head into the room and said, "Mr. Secretary, you're on in three minutes." Immediately, with a hint of regret, the cabinet officer straightened himself; his easy informality disappeared, the banter in the room ceased as his companions recognized the change. The secretary became more serious; he stood straight; he became distant in attitude.

The others in the room noted the change in him and pulled back emotionally, showing their respect. The secretary had now assumed the role of a high government official with the decorum it required. He stood with dignity and reserve; he shook hands in farewell to his friends. Then he left the room to give his speech, entering the auditorium to thunderous applause.

In those few minutes he had shed his role as old friend and assumed his role as a high official of the government. Which then was the real person? Some may insist that it was the informal person, but he was also very much the national leader. His personality was broad enough to encompass both roles.

To say that leadership is a role is not to say that it is thereby neither natural nor honest. Thinking about leadership as a role reminds us that leadership, in large part, is about fulfilling (and exceeding) the expectations of others. Leadership requires a set of skills (described in Chapter 4), of which the most important is the ability to recognize the expectations surrounding you, because they define the role of the leader in the context in which you find yourself.

If you fulfill those expectations, then you are able to lead in those circumstances. It hardly matters whether fulfilling the expectations people have of a leader comes to you easily or with great difficulty, as long as you do it successfully. Whether naturally or with effort, you have become a leader.

Overcoming Personal Obstacles to Leadership

We've observed that not everyone is ideally suited by personality to become effective leaders. Can an introvert become an effective leader? Although we've said that leadership is not a particular personality trait, it is certainly easier for extroverts to play a role that requires interacting with many other people. Yet many introverts are able to learn skills, such as public speaking, that are significant to leadership. Even though introverts may become good at public speaking, it rarely becomes fun for them. They still have to discipline themselves to do it well.

In fact, many effective speakers are much more introverted than is generally known. One of the most famous business leaders of recent years was so fearful of public speaking that while he spoke and gestured with his right hand, he would hold his left arm rigidly at his side, his left hand knotted into a tight fist, reflecting the tension caused by the firm control he was exerting on his whole body to force himself not only to remain in front of his audience, but even to appear to be relaxed as he spoke.

Another very well known CEO, a leader of an enormous firm, would stand behind the curtains of an auditorium before he was to give a talk, so nervous that he sweated profusely, wiping his brow with a handkerchief and almost unable to converse. Then when the introduction was over and he was announced, he'd gather himself together, stride onstage from where he'd been hiding, concealed from the audience's view, face the crowd, and speak so comfortably and informally that people in the audience would think he was completely at ease.

Difficult though it is for an introvert to assume the role of a public leader, it can be done, and often is. It's a matter of the desire to be effective in the role of leader and the self-discipline to accomplish it. Most people who hear and see such a person speak cannot tell the difference between the extrovert who is a natural leader and the introvert who struggles to be perceived as a natural leader.

Another important element of leadership is the exercise of power. In most organizations, leaders use power to mobilize the support and resources to get things done. (See Jeffrey Pfeffer, **Managing with Power: Politics and Influence in Organizations,** Boston: Harvard Business School Press, 1993.) In some ways public speaking and the use of power are almost at the opposite ends of a spectrum of tools of leadership. Public speaking relies on persuasion and rests on logic and emotion to gain support. Power relies on rewards and punishments. There is no distinction between extroverts and introverts in the use of power. But again, some people are naturally comfortable exercising power; others are not at all; and some never will be. Yet all can be leaders. People uncomfortable exercising power can learn to do it—it's a part of what is expected of a leader. It is part of the role.

Whatever a person's natural qualities, he or she can become a leader if sufficient desire is there. For many people it's not easy, and it may be uncomfortable. Nevertheless, each of us can do it if we wish. In fact, as we noted above, many of the

Leadership: How to Lead, How to Live

best leaders in our country have overcome substantial impediments to become effective leaders.

Here we will mention only two. One of America's greatest presidents was crippled as a young man by polio—a wasting disease that attacked many young people before it was finally virtually eliminated by a vaccine. The young man who got polio and lost the use of both his legs, so that he had to move around on crutches, was Franklin Delano Roosevelt—the only American ever elected president for four terms (1932-1945), and the president who led the U.S. successfully through World War II. He was a great leader despite being physically challenged.

In more recent years, one of America's most effective corporate chief executive officers has been Jack Welch of the General Electric Company. Welch has a speech impediment that causes him to stutter; yet he has trained himself to overcome the impediment so that, while CEO, he was able to give speech after speech to present his company to audiences of investors, employees, and customers.

President Roosevelt and Jack Welch both developed such outstanding leadership skills that people began to see them as charismatic. They were not leaders because they were charismatic, but rather the opposite—they seemed charismatic because they were leaders. Similarly, with effort, each of us can become a leader; if we become effective enough as leaders, we are likely to begin to seem charismatic to others.

Starting to Become a Leader

We begin the process of making ourselves leaders by starting with our imaginations. We imagine ourselves as leaders in front of a group of people giving a talk; imagine ourselves in the office suggesting a course of action to our fellow workers; imagine ourselves in a situation of danger or stress pointing the way for others to safety; imagine ourselves in a circumstance of great temptation urging others to take the ethical course. Such incidents are what leadership is about.

But we can imagine more. We can imagine ourselves in a position of continual leadership—perhaps we envision ourselves as president of a company, directing its employees day after day. Perhaps we envision ourselves as director of a not-for-profit organization that helps other people, and it's our responsibility to bring assistance to those in need. We have institutionalized our leadership in a position of authority—a position of leadership!

With imaginings like this in our minds, we can accustom ourselves to the notion of ourselves as leaders of other people. We can begin to acquire the skills that will make us leaders. At first, only we will see ourselves as leaders, but before long, as we act like leaders, others will recognize leadership in us and before we know it, we'll be what we set out to be: real leaders. The first step in this process is mental; the value, and impact, of being able to envision ourselves in these leadership roles can not be overestimated.

To lead is to live dangerously. It's romantic and exciting to think of leadership as inspiring others, taking decisive action, and reaping rich rewards, but leading requires taking risks that can jeopardize one's career and one's personal life.

Political history is full of the tragic stories of people who sought to provide leadership and lost their lives or their freedom as a result. One can find modern examples daily in the news from abroad. In business, people who strive for leadership are sometimes forced out of their firms after losing power struggles to others.

EXECUTIVE SUMMARY 2-2

KEY OBSTACLES TO LEARNING HOW TO LEAD

There are obstacles to leadership, usually of our own making, that we must overcome to be successful leaders:

- Believing that all leaders are born leaders
- Thinking that leadership can't be learned
- Fearing the risks and responsibilities of leadership

---❖---

Leadership requires putting yourself on the line, disrupting the status quo, and bringing hidden conflicts to the surface. And when other people resist and push back, there's a strong temptation to play it safe. Those who choose to lead plunge in, take the risks, and sometimes get burned. (See Ronald A. Heifetz and Marty Linsky, **Leadership on the Line: Staying Alive Through the Dangers of Leading**, Boston: Harvard Business School Press, 2002.)

When we achieve a position of top leadership, the media may become interested in us. The exposure to the broad public can be very good for our organizations, but it can entail risks for us because the media now invades the personal lives of public figures more than before. For example, Presidents Franklin D. Roosevelt and John F. Kennedy both had private lives that involved potential scandal, but the public never knew about these things because the press respected (or protected) their personal lives. Yet, some historians say that America might never have elected those two leaders had the media revealed more about their private lives. The same trend of media scrutiny of the private lives of leaders may begin to reach leaders at other levels than the Presidency. If it does, then leaders in today's world will need to play an outward facing role more than ever, precisely because of the media's increasing invasion of their private lives.

Because there is an element of career and personal danger in exercising leadership, one is likely to be somewhat fearful about reaching for a leadership role. We may be afraid that others will reject us in a leadership role, damaging our self-esteem or the respect others have for us. We may be afraid that we will lose out in a contest for leadership and our careers will suffer. For some, fear may become a paralyzing factor in the advancement of our careers.

The fear of damage to our pride if we seek to be leaders and fail might seem to be the easiest fear to overcome. But we live in an image-conscious society that makes it difficult for most of us to act in a manner consistent with the realization that the only person we have to prove anything to is ourselves.

Many think there is a psychological predisposition in people that makes them leaders. For some this is true – for what we can call natural leaders. But for most it isn't true. The psychological disposition that matters isn't toward leadership itself, but the willingness to play that role. What a person must possess to be a leader is not the leader's psychology, but instead a willingness to play a role. Many of us have the ability, to stand out, to assume the risks and responsibilities, but we fear the role and so choose not to be leaders.

Although fear should not force us to retreat from our goal of becoming a leader, it is a good idea to pause for a bit of self-reflection, which may prove instrumental in developing our character and our capability as leaders. We should take the opportunity to re-evaluate and realistically assess our situation, remaining confident in our goals, being persistent, and pressing on. This is an area where friends and family can be a great source of encouragement and strength.

To triumph over fear and use it to improve ourselves, we must establish checkpoints to ensure that we avoid allowing fear to become a paralyzing factor in our careers. One effective means of doing this is to seek feedback from our superiors, employees, and peers that allows us to change paths quickly if we are heading in the wrong direction.

The founder and CEO of one of America's largest computer retail companies swallowed his pride a few years ago and accepted written evaluations from the people who worked directly for him.

What he found surprised him. He thought that he was an effective leader but feedback told a different story; people found him curt and almost rude. What did he do? He tore down the office wall separating him from other executives and replaced it with a glass wall and a glass door, which he usually leaves open during the day.

CHAPTER REFERENCES:

Heifetz, Ronald A., and Marty Linsky. **Leadership on the Line: Staying Alive Through the Dangers of Leading.** Boston: Harvard Business School Press, 2002.

Pfeffer, Jeffrey. **Managing with Power: Politics and Influence in Organizations.** Boston: Harvard Business School Press, 1993.

ADDITIONAL READINGS:

DePree, Max. **Leadership Is an Art.** New York: Currency, 1989.

Garten, Jeffrey E. **The Mind of the CEO.** Cambridge, MA: Perseus Publishing, 2001.

Leadership: How to Lead, How to Live

Chapter 3

Finding Our Basis For Leadership

You gain strength, courage and confidence by every experience in which you really stop to look fear in the face. You must do the thing you think you cannot do.

- Eleanor Roosevelt, political activist, wife of President Franklin Roosevelt

Leadership: How to Lead, How to Live

In Chapter 2 we saw that leadership can be learned. In this chapter we recognize that people have different bases on which to build a position of leadership.

There are multiple bases for leadership. A person may be accepted as a leader because of her charisma; or because of his expertise; or because she occupies a position of authority; or because he is a success and people want to be successful also; or because people respond to her deep level of commitment; or, finally, because his values resonate with people. We will look at each in turn.

Charisma

In Chapter 1 we noted that many people incorrectly confuse charisma with leadership itself; hence it is no surprise that charisma often serves as a basis for leadership. **Charisma** is a personality characteristic that causes other people to want to follow the charismatic person. It's a unique quality that captures a room, captivates an audience or group, and draws the group together around an individual.

Charisma may involve one's personal style: how she dresses, how he carries himself, her appearance, his demeanor, so that others want to be like him or her, trying to dress as he or she does, assuming the same attitude, frequenting the same places, walking the same way, having the same sort of friends, wearing the same hair styles, listening to the same music. It's charisma that advertisers look for when they are seeking people to endorse their products. For example, a moderately successful tennis player who is very attractive might find herself lured off the tennis courts to be a model, endorsing clothing for manufacturers or retailers. It isn't her tennis playing that has attracted advertisers to her, but rather her charisma—her appearance and bearing—which other people want to emulate.

Charisma can also be the basis of leadership for broader things than style. A tall, handsome man who dresses well and has a regal bearing may be more readily accepted as the head of a corporation or a university than someone with less presence.

For example, it has been written about Warren Harding, president of the United States in the 1920s: "Harding, with his booming voice and classic good looks, simply appeared Presidential...Yet Harding proved to be one of the worst U.S. Presidents." (Diane Brady, *Business Week*, December 27,

2004, p. 26.) Well-qualified candidates are sometimes turned away from top positions because, they are told, "you don't look like a college president," or "you don't look like a corporate CEO." Sometimes discrimination can be a factor in such a rejection; but sometimes it's a judgment that the person lacks those personal qualities that make others want to follow him or her—that he or she lacks charisma.

Expertise

But charisma isn't the only criterion for leadership; and in fact some people with little charisma become effective leaders. **Expertise** is another important basis for leadership. Imagine that a group of people are in the woods, and they suddenly realize that they're lost. When they look around the group, and one woman says she's been in this place before and knows the way out, she suddenly becomes the group's leader. It doesn't matter whether she's charismatic or not—she knows the way.

In exactly this way, expertise or knowledge or experience becomes the basis of leadership—a person becomes the leader because he knows how to do something. This basis for leadership can extend a surprisingly long way. In business, it's not uncommon for the person who heads a large retail store chain to be more than just a good administrator, but an expert in merchandising as well, so that employees and colleagues respect him or her for that expertise. It's the basis of his or her leadership. We sometimes hear people ask, "Who's the top retailer?" or "Who's the top auto guy?" and realize that they mean "Who knows the most about this?" The person is a leader because he or she has the expertise.

Finding Our Basis For Leadership

A Position of Authority

More commonly, people look to someone for leadership because he or she holds a **position of authority.** Thus, a person who is promoted to be the head of a department or a division of a company, or of the company itself, is expected to be a leader—all eyes in the company turn to her for leadership. The expectation of leadership goes with the job.

People sometimes rise to the occasion of an important position and demonstrate considerable leadership. Regarding Charles deGaulle, leader of the French resistance to the Nazis during World War II and later president of France, a close associate wrote: "There was nothing charismatic about his speeches and press conferences. His strength lay…in his authority, not in projecting an attractive image." (Andre Malraux, **Anti-Memoirs,** New York: Henry Holt, 1990, p. 105.) The basis of deGaulle's leadership lay in his positions of authority.

Yet, we must be careful not to confuse leadership with position. We often call the person who heads something its "leader," as if high position and leadership were synonymous. They aren't, however. A person can be in a high position and have no leadership skills and not be accepted as a leader. Although this person may be the boss, he or she is not a leader.

Sometimes a person has a base that gives him leadership (like expertise, achievement, charisma) and so comes to a top position.

Sometimes a person gets a top position (perhaps by being a good administrator) and then has an opportunity to lead, by virtue of his or her position. So causality can work either

51

way: from leadership to a top position, or from a top position to leadership.

When a person attains a high position and isn't a leader, it usually disappoints many people—those who work for him, and perhaps those who selected him. In politics, we elect people to positions of authority. We can evaluate their leadership potential and try to choose leaders. But in business, people do not elect the person for whom they work. Usually, a position is filled by a person of higher rank (for example, the vice president of the company promotes someone to the job of department manager, and the CEO chooses a person for the vice president's job). When that happens, employees look to the new person for leadership skills. Similarly, a person may inherit a position of authority in a family or in a family business. When others then look to that person for leadership, sometimes they find what they're looking for and sometimes they don't.

Sometimes a person coming in to a position of importance has leadership skills and is recognized immediately as a leader. Sometimes she develops the skills of leadership on the job. Sometimes a person doesn't have leadership skills and never acquires them, even though he stays in the position. In a case such as this, the job is then being filled by an administrator. If the job is routine, it may not require leadership skills. As a result, a person may be promoted up a chain of command to the very top job, serving in each position along the way as an administrator but never acquiring leadership skills. Only if the company's environment is very stable and the company only requires day-to-day administration, is the company likely to prosper under such a person. Usually, leadership is required to meet the demands of market change and competition, and without it, a firm is in trouble.

The critical point is that although we expect leadership from a person in a high position, we don't always get it.

A Record of Success

A person may become a leader simply because he or she is successful, and others turn to that person for the secret of **success** for themselves.

Warren Buffett, for example, is not charismatic or an expert at any particular business, nor does he hold a position that causes people to look to him for leadership. However, he is one of the most successful investors the United States has ever seen, and therefore many people look to him for leadership—not only for investing, where he has some expertise, but for a range of topics—because he has been so financially successful. Each year Buffett issues an annual report for his company, Berkshire Hathaway, which is eagerly snapped up and read by countless numbers of people who are not shareholders in the company, but who accept Buffett as a leader.

Donna Shalala lacks many of the characteristics that people would associate with charisma—but she is a strong, dynamic leader and has been both a cabinet member (in the Clinton administration) and the president of several excellent colleges and universities.

Napoleon Bonaparte, once emperor of France, was a great leader in his time. Today he is widely described by historians as charismatic. But Napoleon didn't see himself that way. He was not French, but Corsican; his name was not French, but Italian; he spoke French with an Italian accent; he was small in stature. At the beginning of his military career, he was poorly dressed and clumsy in manners. He did not present himself well in the salons of Paris. No one thought of him as charismatic. Many instead saw him as a buffoon.

But he was a skilled artillerist. By good fortune, he took part in the French siege of Toulon, a port in the south of France that had been occupied by the British, and by careful placement of artillery, forced the English ships to evacuate the harbor, and the English army to depart with them. He was then revered as a hero. Given a poorly equipped army, he invaded northern Italy and won great victories, enriching his troops and the coffers of the French revolutionary government.

Because he had been successful, he became famous. Soldiers wanted to follow him; top government officials turned to him for help; he was given more armies, and more success followed. His fame grew. He was recognized as a leader.

As success followed success, an aura of invincibility grew around him. The small man with the peculiar name and accent came to seem a charismatic leader. Napoleon adapted himself well to the role—he issued flowery proclamations; he gave speeches to inspire his troops (before the battle of the Pyramids outside Cairo, Egypt, he said to his troops, "Soldiers, forty centuries look down on you!"), he wore elegant uniforms, and he carried himself with an air of command.

Yet Napoleon never forgot the source of his leadership. "My power depends on my glory," he once explained to a person who asked why he couldn't give up warfare and become a peaceful leader of the French nation, "and my glory depends upon my victories!" That is, he had to be successful again and again on the battlefield to retain his followers—to retain his leadership.

It is not so different in business and politics today. Leadership is generally accepted from a person who contributes significantly to make a company financially successful or who is able to win elections. Success conveys an aura of leadership.

A High Level of Commitment

An unusually high level of **commitment** to the objectives of a group of people can result in a person being accepted as a leader. The most dramatic examples are probably from warfare; for example, when a group of soldiers hiding from enemy fire behind a knoll or in a trench are suddenly energized by one of their number who leaps up and races forward toward the enemy, the others then, encouraged by his example, rise to follow. It is his courage, his commitment to their common objective that suddenly galvanizes them to action and takes them forward.

Examples from sports come readily to mind also—for example, the soccer player who, in a huddle of the team when it is losing, suddenly overcoming weariness and disappointment, rises with an excited expression of determination and leads the other players back onto the field and into the game.

In business it may be an individual who, after the sales office has lost a major account and is demoralized, comes in the next morning with an idea about how to get a replacement account and quickly gathers followers who are looking for a renewal of commitment.

A Shared Set of Values

People look for leaders among those who share their **values**, to the extent that sometimes nothing more is necessary. Perhaps the most dramatic examples are in politics. In the United States, presidential contenders make great efforts to persuade voters that they are the candidate who shares the values—family, integrity, religion, patriotism—of the voters, believing that many people will give them their votes if they believe a candidate shares their values.

So significant have values become in recent American presidential elections, that political commentators debate whether they have displaced issues as the primary basis for how voters determine which candidate to support. Religious values are becoming more important in some workplaces, so some people seek leadership status partly on the basis of identifying with the religious values of those who choose leaders in the business.

The increasingly important role of values as a basis for leadership may reflect the way people are educated today. Increasingly, we train people to be leaders without training them where to lead. The problem is that leadership skills can be put toward improper objectives. Thus people often look to a person's values rather than his or her leadership skills as an indicator of that person's leadership objectives. (See Joseph L. Badaracco Jr. and Richard R. Ellsworth, **Leadership and the Quest for Integrity**, Boston: Harvard Business School Press, 1993.)

There is more to values as a basis for leadership, however, than simply what they point to as likely objectives of leadership. Shared values in an organization facilitate effective leadership. Values are commitments or beliefs that

Finding Our Basis For Leadership

drive behavior. Commonly held values create favorable conditions for resolving controversies. A set of values embedded in the way people work permits cooperation and leadership across demographic, cultural, and organizational divides.

Here is a set of values upon which professional and business cooperation can be built today:

1. A commitment to change

2. A recognition that financial values are not all that matters

3. An acceptance of personal responsibility for outcomes

4. A bias for action

5. A commitment to ethical behavior

These five values constitute the basis for cooperation among people in an organization or community. They do not conflict with the more sophisticated versions of most of the world's religions and cultures. They are not American values projected onto the global stage where they are challenged by those of other civilizations. Instead, they emerge out of the confluence of European, African, Asian, and American cultures. They are excellent business values that have broad application.

A commitment to change recognizes that too much is changing in the outside world for things to remain unchanged in the company. A commitment to change means that we are proactive, not reactive, in our attitude toward change.

A recognition that financial values are not all that matters is a way of rejecting exploitation and trying to promote meaningful non-pecuniary aspects of life.

An acceptance of personal responsibility for outcomes is a way of insisting that people truly engage in attempting to bring about meaningful change.

A bias for action insists that people do more than just talk.

A commitment to ethical behavior is so important to some people that it is all they mean when they refer to values-based leadership.

These values seem trivial to some in places where they are largely accepted. However, many people do not accept them at all, including some who give them lip service. Honestly embraced, these values provide a basis for advancement in the world. They become the basis for partnerships. These values help create an environment that fosters effective leadership. The new leadership is in the network of committed people.

Some people consider values so important as a basis for leadership that they divide leadership into only two categories: personality-based and values-based.

Caring

A final basis for leadership is **caring,** or empathy—the feeling people have that someone is deeply concerned about them personally, is in some fundamental way one of them. Followers identify with a leader when they feel this way. The source of the identification need not be demographic (he or she is one of our age group, or ethnic group, or religious sect), but is rather the emotional conviction of the followers that the leader understands and cares about them and what happens to them. Caring is the basis of an emotional connection between leader and followers.

Several years ago a high school teacher in a particularly difficult inner-city school won the national teaching award in the United States. In his acceptance speech he explained that before he could provide educational leadership to his classes, he had to gain their confidence. That is, the students had to accept him as a leader. To gain their confidence, he had to show them that he cared about them as individuals. Only then would the students be prepared to learn from him; only then did they care how much he knew and could potentially teach them. "Students don't care how much you—the teacher—know," he said, "until they know how much you care!"

This is not only true of students. Many people will not accept a person as a leader unless they believe that he or she cares about them—that he or she has their best interests at heart.

We have identified seven major bases for leadership. (See Executive Summary 3-1). Seven is a large number, and it follows that leadership comes in a remarkable variety of packages. An individual leader may embody one or any combination of these bases for leadership. There are many different combinations that explain a person's leadership appeal. For example, when Bill Clinton ran for his second term in the White House in 1996, political commentators said his appeal to the American electorate rested on a strong combination of charisma, authority (he was already the president), commitment, values (shared with a large section of the electorate), and unusually strong emotional resonance.

In contrast, when George W. Bush sought re-election in 2004, political commentators described his successful appeal to a majority of the electorate as based largely upon commitment (to winning the war against terrorism) and values that were widely shared.

Bill Clinton and George W. Bush are from different political parties and have different bases for their leadership, but both have been very effective in being chosen by the American people to be leaders of the nation.

EXECUTIVE SUMMARY 3-1

SEVEN BASES FOR LEADERSHIP

There are seven bases upon which a person can be recognized as a leader:

1. Charisma: People want to do what I do because I do it.
2. Expertise: I know how to get us out of this or how to accomplish something others want done.
3. Authority and position: People look to me for guidance because I am in a position of authority with respect to them.
4. Success: People want to share in my success.
5. Commitment: People know that I care very much about what they care about.
6. Values: People know that I believe in what they believe.
7. Empathy: People believe that I understand and care about them.

It is not only politics. Similar situations occur in business. A person may be chosen to head a great company because of one or a combination of the bases for leadership. For example, the board of directors of a large retail discount store chain sometimes chooses a CEO who is a great merchandiser—that is, for his expertise; but at a later time the board may choose another CEO for her charisma (counting on her to inspire employees and excite investors); and at yet a third time, it may choose another CEO for his commitment to a new strategic course for the company. And, of course, at any time the person chosen to lead the company might embody not just one but several of the bases for leadership.

Does it follow, we might ask, that the more bases for leadership a person has, the better leader he or she is likely to be? Probably not. For example, a person who is superbly successful may be the best leader a firm ever had, despite lacking charisma, expertise, or others of the bases listed above. However, in Chapter 4 we will see that the more leadership qualities a leader has, the better and more successful a leader is likely to be.

The bases for leadership are not, generally, the same as the qualities of leadership. Being in a position of authority is often a basis for leadership, but it is not a quality of leadership. Expertise is often a basis for leadership, but it is not a quality of leadership—many leaders lack detailed expertise but instead are generalists. Success is a basis for leadership, but it is not a quality of leadership—many leaders try hard and are not successful but are accepted by their followers.

In U.S. history, for example, George Washington was accepted as leader of the revolutionary armies despite years of repeated defeat; ultimately Washington won, but his leadership didn't depend on success but on other bases, particular expertise and commitment, that long-predated success on the battlefield. General Robert E. Lee, beloved by many people of the southern states despite his defeat by the North on the battlefield, is another good example. Lee was a great leader, but in the end, unsuccessful.

Values are a basis for leadership, but not a quality of leadership, although, as we shall see, ethics are a quality of leadership. Values are a basis for ethics, but people choose a leader because he or she expresses the same sort of values they have, not because the person is ethical in his or her behavior. Empathy can be a basis for leadership, but it is not a key quality of leadership. Many leaders do not possess it, and it is not necessary for successful leadership (although some leaders make empathy part of their overall leadership style). Perhaps the world would be better off if more leaders possessed greater empathy—an interesting topic for discussion.

Charisma and commitment are different. They are both bases for leadership and qualities of a leader. Charisma is so strongly associated in our minds with leadership that many of us have trouble thinking of leadership as anything else. If a person is charismatic, many of us think of that person as a leader immediately. We expect our leaders to have charisma; we are disappointed when they don't. Hence, when we discuss the qualities of leadership, we'll often find ourselves talking about charisma.

Commitment is similar, though less salient. Commitment to an objective can be the basis for leadership, and we shall see that it is an expected quality of a leader, even if the leader's basis for leadership is something other than commitment.

An effective leader steadily enlarges his or her base of leadership. When the initial base is a position of authority, a leader may gain in personal confidence and stature. She becomes charismatic, and adds charisma to her leadership base. He becomes successful, and adds success to his leadership base.

Alternatively, if her original base was expertise, she may rise to a position of authority, adding that to her base; and with success, add that to her base. Steadily his base expands, deepens, and diversifies until it is unassailable.

Leading from Behind

We've identified seven bases upon which we can build our role of leadership. In each instance the leader is at the front of his or her organization setting a direction and leading the way. But there is another approach to leadership: leading from behind.

In this case the leader is not at the top of an organization's pyramid but somewhere in the middle or even at the bottom. The leader is not outspoken and aggressive, but soft-spoken and humble yet energetic and determined. The leader acts by persuasion and example but cannot command or direct in any way. All the skills and qualities of leadership that we will review in later chapters can be used by a person leading from behind. This is a nontraditional view of leadership, however, but one that I think many of us will find very encouraging.

FREQUENTLY ASKED QUESTIONS:

Question: *Contrasting a leader with an administrator (as opposed to contrasting a leader with a manager), and conceiving of leadership as a role are intriguing new approaches but a bit confusing. Perhaps people can play the role of leadership to varying degrees, but isn't specific expertise required for one to be an effective leader? For example, the ability to delegate; to be detail-oriented yet keep the big picture in mind; to inspire; to play the visionary; and to manage people, expectations, and projects are all skills I believe a good leader must possess.*

Answer: Perhaps, but some of these skills are administrative skills, not leadership skills, and therefore characterize a good manager but not a leader (specifically, the ability to delegate, to be detail-oriented yet keep the big picture in mind, and to manage people, expectations, and projects). You may be using the term "leader" to mean a person in a high position, in which case you are confused about what a leader is. A person can be a leader without being in a position of authority. When you think of leadership as a role, then it is clearly independent of a position of authority, and can be exercised at any level of an organization and in any sort of setting.

Question: *When you say that some people are better at playing the leadership role than others, are you suggesting that they are equipped with these aptitudes?*

Answer: No. Some people work harder at leadership than others, and as a result they do it better. Also, some people have more natural aptitude for leadership, so it's easier for them. However, others, without the natural aptitude, can learn to be excellent leaders.

Finding Our Basis For Leadership

Question: *I agree that self-control and discipline can help one overcome certain aspects of the leadership role (e.g., public speaking in the spotlight), but how does a manager effectively motivate an employee if he/she just does not understand human behavior?*

Answer: A good question. But motivation using incentives, rewards, and punishment is an administrative skill, not a leadership skill. Inspiring people to work without financial motivation is a leadership skill.

Question: *Can self-control and discipline enable one to become a better leadership "role player" in all circumstances?*

Answer: Yes. They can also help prevent a person from being carried away by success as a leader into unethical directions.

———❖———

Leadership: How to Lead, How to Live

CHAPTER REFERENCES:

Badaracco, Joseph L. Jr., and Richard R. Ellsworth. **Leadership and the Quest for Integrity.** Boston: Harvard Business School Press, 1993.

Malraux, Andre. **Anti-Memoirs.** New York: Henry Holt, 1990

ADDITIONAL READINGS:

Bstan-Dzin-Rgya-Mtsho. **A Simple Path: Basic Buddhist Teachings by His Holiness the Dalai Lama.** London: Thorsons Publishers, 2000.

Mandela, Nelson. **The Long Walk to Freedom: The Autobiography of Nelson Mandela.** Boston: Back Bay Books, 1995.

Mother Teresa. **Mother Teresa: In My Own Words.** New York: Gramercy, 1997.

Whyte, David. **The Heart Aroused: Poetry and the Preservation of the Soul in Corporate America.** New York: Currency, 1996.

Leadership: How to Lead, How to Live

PART II

THE CENTRAL ELEMENTS OF LEADERSHIP

Leadership: How to Lead, How to Live

Chapter 4

Being a Successful Leader

To grasp and hold a vision, that is the very essence of successful leadership—not only on the movie set where I learned it, but everywhere.

- Ronald Reagan, U.S. President

Leadership: How to Lead, How to Live

In the first part of this book we defined leadership, saw that it can be learned, and identified the different bases on which a person's position of leadership can be built. In this chapter we begin a discussion that will continue throughout Part 2 about how to be a successful leader.

We've said before that leadership is a complex and multifaceted thing. In this chapter we turn to some of the most important facets of leadership. We identify the nine key qualities of a leader and the five central skills of leadership.

———————❖———————

Nine Key Qualities of Leadership

Leading, as we have seen, can rest on several bases. The actual work of leadership requires specific qualities and skills to translate those qualities into action—and effectiveness (i.e., results).

The nine key qualities of leadership—passion, decisiveness, conviction, integrity, adaptability, emotional toughness, emotional resonance, self-awareness, humility—are found in varying levels in given individuals, but all of them can be acquired (to some extent) by conscious choice.

Passion

Passion has several meanings, but one of them is boundless enthusiasm. A passionate leader displays his feelings or emotions for his work, and therefore is perceived to be deeply involved and certain of his role and direction. Passion is something we are all capable of. We are free to employ it whenever we want in relation to whatever we want. But we should be sure to employ it in constructive directions.

Passion is important in the leader of a large organization—it is essential in an entrepreneur.

"No one works the seemingly endless hours, days, weeks, months, and years it takes to get a business off the ground," said Dan Meyers, who created First Marblehead Corporation and led it to become a New York Stock Exchange-listed firm in 2003, "simply because it is an interesting business challenge." In this brief comment, Mr. Meyers encapsulated the difference between top leadership in a large organization and in an entrepreneurial start-up, between the CEO and the entrepreneur.

Great as the commitment is of the big company leader, even greater is that of the entrepreneur. Meyers goes on to identify an entrepreneur as a person obsessed with a single mission—whose passion dominates everything else in her life. The leader of a large, established company in contrast ordinarily has much less passion for what he does and has a much greater breadth of interest. Passion is not usually the central quality of the leader of a large and long-established organization.

Passion is such an important quality in a leader that it is often mistaken for charisma. A leader may have such passion for his company and such energy associated with it, that it is almost hypnotic to others and perceived as a form of charisma. Yet passion is not charisma; nor does passion necessarily become leadership. A scientist can be passionate about her research, yet seclude herself for years in her laboratory.

Decisiveness

A leader is called upon to take charge, and this requires decisiveness. Great leaders have the presence of mind to make decisions under intense stress, and to do so under the pressure of time, with limited information, in ambiguous situations, and with the knowledge that their decisions carry heavy consequences.

The ability to quickly assess a situation and take decisive action is an important leadership attribute. A leader is able to handle high degrees of uncertainty and use personal intuition to act on imperfect information. A leader can respond to crises or threats without suffering from analysis paralysis—effective leaders recognize that spending more time analyzing a situation often is not commensurate with the resulting benefit.

It is important to note that sometimes leaders make the wrong decisions. Leaders must be able to live with their decisions without succumbing to feelings of regret about mistakes or lost opportunities. Leaders have great demands on their time so those who are sluggish in their decisions often fail to act. Inaction can signal to others unsuitability for leadership.

Throughout history exceptional individuals who otherwise would have been effective leaders have been ineffective due to indecisiveness. However, decisions must not be so hasty and poorly thought out that they lead to disaster.

Quick decisions must be tempered with patient wisdom so that the leader makes an ill-informed decision *only* when it is critical to act and when the risks of waiting for additional information far outweigh the benefits.

Conviction

Conviction is an important underlying quality that every leader must have—conviction about her role as a leader and about the purpose or objective that she and the organization are trying to achieve.

A leader must perform a host of different functions within an organization, including:

- Communicating a vision

- Energizing people via example and inspiration

- Making difficult decisions

To be effective in carrying out these responsibilities, a leader must show conviction. A leader cannot convincingly communicate a vision or objective if he is not committed to it himself. To inspire people, a leader must first earn her credibility and demonstrate that she has personal conviction about the goals that she is trying to inspire people to achieve. Finally, to make difficult decisions that benefit the organization and steer it toward its stated goal, a leader's judgment and instincts must be informed by a conviction about the desired end.

EXECUTIVE SUMMARY 4-1

NINE KEY QUALITIES OF LEADERSHIP

There are nine key qualities that a leader should possess:

1. Passion
2. Decisiveness
3. Conviction
4. Integrity
5. Adaptability
6. Emotional toughness
7. Emotional resonance
8. Self-awareness
9. Humility

Integrity

A very important quality for the true leader is integrity. Integrity is the type of honesty that leads someone to do the right thing even when no one else is present. Although often operating below the surface, integrity is surprisingly apparent to others, and it earns respect. Other qualities of leadership, including charisma and decisiveness, unless coupled with integrity, lead to the sort of evil doings that we have insisted do not constitute authentic leadership. Other leadership qualities comprise the motor that steers the organization towards a goal; integrity is the driver which sets the direction.

Adaptability

The ability to adapt to changing circumstances is an essential attribute for a leader. Effective leaders refer to "learning to embrace change" and "being resilient" as top attributes of a good leader.

How does a leader effectively adapt to change? First, he recognizes when there has been a meaningful change in the internal or external environment. This involves actively listening to others (especially those within his organization) and persistently monitoring the external environment. Then, based upon input about change, the leader must determine whether to make a change in the activities of his unit. If a change is required, then the leader must develop a new direction and communicate it clearly to his organization. Finally, he must energize others to move toward the new objective. This may be done with the tools of a leader, including vision and inspiration, or those of an administrator, including incentives and rewards. If the response to the change is insufficient, the leader must recognize this at an early stage, admit he or she was wrong, pick up the pieces, and move on. This process of constant review and adjustment to change should involve self-reflection as well.

Many of the worst leaders are continually uncertain and make repeated course corrections to overcompensate for small changes. Nothing is more frustrating to followers than when their leader is changing her mind or appears uncertain. Followers are then afraid to commit time or energy to any course of action. They will wait until the leader has made up her mind, which often has a negative effect on the efficiency and effectiveness of the organization.

Emotional Toughness

Leaders need to be emotionally tough. They are constantly challenged internally and externally for better or for worse.

Therefore, leaders who display their emotions easily risk appearing out of control. Emotional displays can trigger negative word-of-mouth as easily as charisma triggers positive word-of-mouth.

When the top executive of a large division of a huge telecom company came to the office one day and noticed a spot on his shirt, he frowned. Subordinates mistook his concern about a matter of appearance for displeasure about the state of the business. When a top executive of a bank got a headache one day before a major meeting and frowned, subordinates took it as an indication that the bank was in trouble.

Emotional Resonance

Emotional resonance is another quality of leadership; it is the ability to mobilize the emotions of other people to drive them toward certain goals. As such, it is thought by many to be a key element of charisma. But it is different from charisma. Many charismatic leaders have no empathy for others, and therefore no emotional resonance.

Empathy involves an understanding of the emotions of others, and may include a sincere caring about their welfare—but with or without caring, it is the central component of emotional resonance. The basic notion underlying the perception of emotional resonance as a key quality of leadership is that human beings react more to their emotions than to their interests—more to excitement than to money; more to a cause than to a paycheck.

Effective leaders make connections with other people; they have an ability to marshal people's energies in a positive way and to bring people together for a common purpose. (See Daniel Goleman, Richard Boyatzis, and Annie McKee, **Primal Leadership: Learning to Lead with Emotional Intelligence**, Boston: Harvard Business School Press, 2004.) A leader's emotions are said to be contagious within an organization, and so they must resonate with enthusiasm with the other people if the organization is to thrive. In this view business leadership isn't about setting strategy but rather about driving the emotions of other people in the right direction.

Self-Awareness

Different leaders have different definitions of success (see Chapter 14.) They have followed different career paths, and have different personalities and mixes of leadership skills and qualities. But most share one important common quality: self-awareness.

Self-awareness expresses itself along three dimensions. First, a self-aware leader knows his purpose in life. Second, a self-aware leader recognizes her style and the basis of her leadership. Third, a self-aware leader recognizes his strengths and weaknesses and seeks other people who complement both. Self-awareness is key to staying true to ourselves and finding our own sweet spots: for each of us the intersection between our personalities, aspirations, and environment.

Self-awareness involves recognizing one's own strengths and weaknesses. A leader is like the leader of a band: He knows what he is good at and is able to fill the gaps in his ability with appropriate people. Knowing one's true abilities comes with self-reflection: the ability to look at yourself honestly and admit your strengths and flaws. Often, would-be leaders fall into the trap of thinking they are good at everything. They are not, and are likely not to be leaders at all.

The ability to consistently and effectively be self-aware plays an important part in the development of leaders over time. Self-awareness allows leaders to assess how up to date they are, and when they fall behind to catch up by various means of learning. Thus, they stay relevant to their organization and industry. It also allows them to be more focused in regard to their own developmental needs. Individuals with high levels of self-awareness are sometimes more flexible in their leadership styles because they recognize when they are inadequate in a particular area. They can then focus on shoring up the necessary skills.

Humility

A leader can only provide direction if she truly understands the interests of her constituents. This ultimately means putting her personal interests and ego aside and truly serving the people who have accepted her in a position of leadership. Leadership in this view is not related to power, but to providing a self-sacrificing service for her followers. This even applies in the business world. A humble leader delegates a considerable amount to people who report to her and expends great effort to enable them to perform well. This may involve the style of management labeled GEM (Goals, Empowerment, Measurement), which encourages considerable delegation of authority to employees in their work (see Mills, **Principles of Management**).

A leader is always thinking of the interests of her team, while understanding the final consequences of her decisions, and thereby puts herself and her employees on the road to success.

The importance of humility is often overlooked, particularly in light of competing claims for other leadership qualities such as decisiveness and charisma. Humility does not imply that a leader lacks decisiveness, resolve, and confidence, but instead that he possesses these qualities in such depth that he doesn't need to create an illusion of competence through arrogance and showmanship. A humble leader is so confident in substance that he does not need to self-promote through style.

Asian societies stress the virtue of humility; for example, one of the most popular Korean aphorisms is, "as the rice becomes ripe in the autumn field, the plant starts to bend down its head and gently move to the wind."

The suggestion is that a person can be an effective leader while treasuring the virtue of humility. The expression of confidence on the surface can sometimes imply insecurity, defense or immaturity resulting from not being fully ripe as a mature person.

Five Central Skills of Leadership

It is not enough for leaders to possess the qualities of leadership. They must also connect qualities with actions so the result is performance. (David Ulrich, Jack Zenger, and Norman Smallwood, **Results-Based Leadership**, Boston: Harvard Business School Press, 1999.)

What fills this gap? It is the application of leadership skills. Only by employing these skills can leaders make real the promises and goals they have established.

EXECUTIVE SUMMARY 4-2

FIVE CENTRAL SKILLS OF LEADERSHIP

There are five central skills important to successful leadership:

1. Defining a leader's vision

2. Setting an example

3. Inspiring others

4. Seeing previously unrecognized capabilities in others

5. Establishing a supportive organizational culture

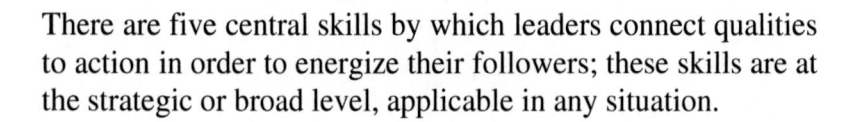

———————❖———————

There are five central skills by which leaders connect qualities to action in order to energize their followers; these skills are at the strategic or broad level, applicable in any situation.

They are the type of skills a leader needs at any level of an organization and in settings in which there is no organization (such as running for political office or leading a group of people in a community project). In Chapter 5 we'll examine operational skills, including those, for example, used within a business organization or a governmental agency.

Defining a Leader's Vision

An effective leader must have a vision of the future—a notion of where the organization he or she is leading should be going. The mission of the organization becomes making the vision a reality.

Perhaps the best vision that has ever been articulated for a large and complex organization is the vision of the National Aeronautics and Space Administration (NASA) in the 1960s—to land a human being on the moon and return them safely. The agency then tied its mission directly to the vision.

Why was NASA's vision of a person on the moon a great vision? First, it was clear and understandable to all. NASA employees, the members of Congress who appropriated money for NASA, the general public who paid taxes to fund NASA—everyone could comprehend exactly what the vision was, and could understand NASA's mission by familiarity with its vision.

Second, the vision involved a real stretch. No human being had ever before walked on the surface of the moon. No nation had even tried to put a person on the moon; up to then, the technology didn't exist to transport a group of people to the moon and bring them back alive. To accomplish the mission involved an enormous amount of creative effort. So great was the reach that even today many people in the world do not believe that the United States actually put a man on the moon several decades ago.

They believe that the whole thing is mere propaganda, and the films that show an astronaut walking on the surface of the moon are merely Hollywood special effects—that is, a lie. But in fact, a man walked on the surface of the moon; the mission was accomplished; the vision was realized. The challenge was overcome.

Third, not only was the vision a stretch for NASA, but it was ultimately something that could be done. It is crucial that a vision and the mission that derives from it be doable—otherwise, if it is merely a dream that cannot be accomplished, then the organization will become demoralized in failing to accomplish it. For this reason, establishing a proper vision and mission is a subtle art—it is not easy to get right. NASA has not had as effective a vision of its future since a man walked on the moon. Its mission has been poorly articulated. It has been difficult to determine whether the agency has been successful. The national leadership has been unable to define a new vision as compelling as the old one.

Why Vision Matters

In business, visions are important to inspire employees to action, to direct their action in a specific way, and to excite investors. Corporate visions are often of a directly competitive nature. When the Japanese equipment maker Kubota was rapidly growing, it established as its vision "beat Caterpillar" —the American firm which at the time was the world leader in manufacturing construction equipment. A CEO of a large retail chain store might have the vision that in ten years her company will be Wal-Mart's largest and most competitive rival. Note that the vision goes beyond mere financial success. For a CEO to say that her vision for her firm is to be a profitable business is not adequate. It's very important for a company to be profitable, but in itself, profitability is too limited to constitute a vision.

If the organization is a start-up business, then the entrepreneur who leads it must know what he or she is trying to build. Investors always demand this; if an entrepreneur can't describe clearly where he expects the firm to be in five years if it is successful, then investors are likely to question the effectiveness of his leadership and will decide not to invest. An entrepreneur might say, for example, that his company is building an Internet search capability. But this is only a description of the type of business activity he's in. He might add that he wants to be the biggest such firm—but that's only an aspiration, not a vision. But suppose he says that in five years his firm will have built the most customer-friendly online store in the world: That's a vision.

The Apple Vision

A famous example of an effective business vision was that of Apple Computer when it was a new company trying to produce and sell the world's first personal computers (then called "micro" computers).

At that time (in the late 1970s and early 1980s), computers were huge machines operated by specialists, housed in special climate-controlled rooms called "glass houses," and not accessible to the ordinary computer user. A person who wished to use a computer typed out a set of instructions on a set of cards (not playing cards but instruction cards) and gave them to a clerk who gave them to the operators of the computer, who then later returned the processed cards to the person who had submitted them. It was a time-consuming, imperfect, expensive system.

Apple set out to change all this. The vision of the company, as imagined by its founders (especially Steven Jobs, its first CEO) was to take computers out of the glass houses and put one on the desk of every person. It was, if you will, to democratize the computer. This was a great vision, for the same reasons that NASA's vision of a person on the moon was a great vision.

The Apple vision was understood by all; it was a stretch; it could be accomplished with significant effort. Apple accomplished the vision. (However, IBM ultimately walked away with most of the personal computer business, and then clones took most of the business away from IBM—two follow-on stories that don't concern us here.)

Another key leadership skill is setting an example for others: how to accomplish a key task, commitment to a mission, courage in the face of adversity, or how to behave in any of a number of other situations. The core of setting an example is to get followers to realize that if their leader can do something, then they can also, and then to get them to give it a try. Unlike visions and missions, examples set by others are familiar to all of us from personal experience early in our lives.

A person can instill desirable qualities in members of the team and organization by exhibiting these qualities in himself or herself. The most inspirational and motivational leaders are those who are inspired and motivated themselves. Where there is a positive and energetic leader, there is usually a positive and energetic culture. Positive examples show employees that their leader is not going to expect them to do anything that he or she wouldn't do. This is very important in establishing credibility and trust for the leader of an organization.

Leading by example challenges the leader to always consider whether or not the qualities and values he or she is exhibiting are those that he or she would want in the company. In decision-making, it pushes the leader to contemplate how he or she would feel on the receiving end. Leading by example is an excellent way for a leader to better understand his or her employees and learn to be a more equitable leader.

Inspiring Others

Jack Welch, former CEO of the General Electric Company, one of America's largest and most successful businesses, once told a group of managers, "No matter how good you are at our business, unless you can energize other people, you are no good to the General Electric Company as a leader." He meant that an administrator who was a good businessperson was valuable to GE in that capacity, but unless he or she was able to inspire others to action on behalf of the company, to energize them in the tasks they performed, then he or she wasn't a leader.

Welch's comment makes it clear that leadership is about others. It's not the work we do as individuals (the business term is "individual contributor") that is important in a leader's role, but what he or she can get others to do by way of example or inspiration or other skills we will identify below. Leaders can inspire others with words or actions.

Seeing Previously Unrecognized Capabilities in Others

Several years ago a team of students from a small high school in a mountain state came in second in a national math contest. People from that team went on to important careers all over the nation. How did it happen that they did so well in the contest, and later did so well in their own careers?

The answer was found in the leadership of a single teacher—the math teacher in that small town's high school. It was she who convinced a group of her students that if they would work hard, they could win contests against students from the big high schools of much bigger cities and states, and from the wealthy preparatory schools—all of whom competed in the national math contest. "She saw in us," one of her students remembered gratefully years later, "potential that we didn't know we had."

This is one of the most important gifts of the leader—to awake in others the desire to accomplish great things and the conviction that with hard work they can succeed. Leadership requires creating an environment that affords those uncertain of their capability every opportunity to get in the game.

This story shows that it isn't what a leader herself does (the teacher didn't participate in the math contest), but what she influences others to do that is the key to leadership. It cannot be emphasized too strongly: Leadership is about others, not about us. The leader's function is to bring out latent ability and commitment in others.

One of us might have a good friend who has been languishing in dead-end jobs for years. He's intelligent, persuasive, and well liked...three noteworthy qualities. But due to his lack of professional success he has begun to doubt his abilities, rationalized his misfortunes, and settled for menial employment that offers little reward (personal or financial).

As leaders, we should help him pursue his goals because of his potential for great impact on our community. Although he'll ultimately need to make a leap on his own, sitting idle and allowing his talent to go unrecognized and undeveloped would be neglecting our duties as leaders.

Establishing a Supportive Organizational Culture

Leaders do not always have a formal role in an organization (sometimes they lead others in informal settings), but when they do—as in business, government, or not-for-profit organizations—then it is an important part of their role to establish a climate in which people can perform well. We call the behavioral climate in an organization its "culture." Sometimes cultures encourage hard work and accomplishment; such cultures allow leaders to energize people for the purposes of the organization. Sometimes cultures do not encourage hard work and accomplishment—they undercut the efforts of a leader to energize others.

One example of a non-constructive culture is a school in which people who study and work hard to get good grades are mocked and ridiculed. This is a dysfunctional culture for learning.

Similar dysfunctional cultures sometimes exist in business. People who work hard and try to get ahead are mocked and ridiculed, and sometimes sabotaged. It's a leader's responsibility to develop, as much as possible, a functional culture. This can be done by example (and is one reason so many bosses come early to work and leave late), by incentives and rewards, or by driving out people who try to undermine a functional culture.

A culture that works well with good leadership can sometimes become dysfunctional when the quality of leadership declines. This happened in what was once America's best-respected and largest accounting firm: Arthur Andersen. The firm was more than one hundred years old and for most of that time had had a reputation for absolute integrity, when it was charged in 2002 by the U.S. Department of Justice with criminal obstruction of justice; in a very short time the firm collapsed and disappeared, putting some 38,000 people out of work.

What happened was that the leadership ceased to champion integrity, and the firm's employees went along with new and dishonest practices. Barbara Lee Toffler, who ran Andersen's ethics consulting practice, wrote: "It was a culture in which everyone followed the rules and the leader. When the rules and leaders stood for decency and integrity, the lockstep culture was the key to competence and respectability. But when ...the leaders changed direction, the culture of conformity led to disaster." (Barbara Lee Toffler, **Final Accounting: Ambition, Greed and the Fall of Arthur Andersen,** New York: Random House, 2003, p. 34.)

In recent years our research has identified four distinct types of cultures in American firms:

- Stagnant
- Crisis-driven
- Continuously improving
- Reaching for excellence

Briefly, a **stagnant** culture is one of routine, inertia, lack of imagination, and little effort, and is dysfunctional for high performance. A **crisis-driven** culture is responsive only when an emergency arises; at other times it is stagnant. Americans have borrowed the concept of the **continuously improving** culture from the Japanese, who seem to have invented it. This is a behavioral environment in which all people are steadily trying to make small, incremental improvements in the efficiency and effectiveness of business activities. Over time such a culture builds up strong productivity and performance.

Finally, many decades ago American companies developed the concept of the **excellent organization**. "The search for excellence," was one of the three founding values of the IBM Corporation (the other two were "respect for the individual," and "the best service"). The search for excellence became a mantra for the efforts to improve the performance of American firms in the 1980s and 1990s, and continues to this day. A leader facilitates the search for excellence in many ways, including rewarding those who practice excellence in all aspects of an organization's work.

A leader must be aware of the culture of his or her organization, and seek continually to improve it, or if it is already excellent, to maintain it at a high level. Organizational culture is always present whether or not a leader deliberately tries to craft a culture. By articulating what the company expects from employees and what employees can expect from working at the company, then people who are a proper fit for the organizational culture are more likely to be attracted to the company.

Working With the Culture

Because a culture of some sort always exists, a leader should work at making it as constructive as possible. If it is dysfunctional, it should be explicitly changed; if it is functional, it must be maintained or improved. Acting on the culture explicitly means identifying it directly and trying to make it different, if necessary, and always better. Many administrators inherit a corporate culture and let it evolve without any overt direction. This is a big mistake, because it may evolve in a dysfunctional direction; and even if it simply stagnates, an opportunity for building a better organization is lost.

All organizations have dominant cultures. A large firm with a dysfunctional culture is a very difficult environment for a well-meaning administrator or leader. An administrator copes as best he or she can; a leader goes much further.

A leader in charge of the whole company tries to change the culture. A leader in charge of a unit of the company, such as a division or a department, tries to create an alternative culture that is supportive of top performance within the unit (a "subculture," so to speak). It is possible to develop functional departments within dysfunctional organizations—although it is a difficult challenge to leadership.

There are two common culture-related pitfalls a leader should attempt to avoid. First, a leader should not overcomplicate the culture by introducing complex mission and vision statements which initially cause confusion and result in total disregard. A leader should ask only that everyone be clearly dedicated to a singular, simple mission (or vision): broadly stated, to build the business by doing one's part to serve the customer.

Second, a leader should not try to portray an organization's culture as something it is not, for example, with slide presentations and glossy handbooks that offer a picture of the perfect company. When that happens, employees often become disillusioned when they begin their jobs and quickly come to realize that everything is not "as advertised." The proper way to lead in the development of a supportive culture is through simplicity and honesty about what the culture is.

Five Styles of Leadership

In all countries the dominant social culture gives a certain flavor to leadership roles. We may call different flavors "styles" of leadership. The United States has a large and complex society; and so rather than one dominant style of leadership, you will find five common styles of leadership.

They are drawn from the most favored qualities or skills of leadership in the U.S. (The five leadership styles a person most often encounters in the U.S. are listed in Executive Summary 4-3.)

Of course there are nuances and shadings to these styles added by the personalities of the leaders who employ them. Some leaders adjust their style depending on the situation.

EXECUTIVE SUMMARY 4-3

FIVE STYLES OF LEADERSHIP

There are five significant styles of leadership in the U.S.:

1. Commanding: decisive

2. Visionary: focused on distant rewards

3. Authentic: ethical, fair

4. Supportive: coaching and supporting others

5. Demagogic: exciting others via extreme emotionalism

The most common leadership style in the U.S. is that of the commanding leader, a person decisive in his or her actions, firm in his or her commitments. Americans believe in individual leadership: They distrust committee decisions; they want quick action. So they seek out leaders who appear to be decisive—who exude an air of command.

Visionary, authentic, and supportive styles of leadership are less common, but do exist. Entrepreneurs are often visionary leaders, as are political officeholders.

Entrepreneurs promise much to employees and investors; politicians promise much to voters.

The executives of large firms sometimes espouse an authentic style of leadership. Authenticity relates to high ethical standards. When Reginald Jones was CEO of General Electric during the 1970s, he described himself as a steward of the firm for its stakeholders—employees, customers, suppliers, and shareholders. A deeply religious man, he drew the concept of stewardship from his faith. He chose Jack Welch to replace him as CEO; Welch adopted a different style, that of the commanding leader.

Some people, upon reaching high positions, prefer not to lead in as decisive a manner as they did on the climb to the top. So they surround themselves with strong people and delegate extensively.

Ahman Kathrada, a leader of the South African anti-apartheid movement quotes Nelson Mandela as follows: "True leaders allow the most nimble to move to the front of the pack, while helping those who are slower keep pace, all the while leading from behind."

Finally, a word about the demagogic style of leadership. A certain amount of emotional conviction is required in a leader. However, some leaders take it much too far, arousing audiences (large or small) to an emotional fervor. Many Americans enjoy emotional experiences; there is a strong market for inspirational speakers in U.S. business life, and a strong preference for emotional preachers in our churches. Europeans, however, are wary of emotionalism. Hitler and Mussolini were emotional speakers who employed their leadership skills to destructive ends. Europeans were much closer to those magnetic but evil personalities, and suffered from the consequences of their actions; they are understandably more suspicious of extreme emotion employed in business and public life.

Many Americans regard European business executives and politicians as bland and unexciting—there is a reason for this, as we have seen-a solid reason grounded in historical experience.

An important set of questions in today's increasingly interconnected business and political world is whether or not the American commanding, decisive style of leadership is a valid approach in other societies? Will globalization make the commanding style more common, or will multi-national organizations and companies and governments of other nations tend towards more collaborative leadership models?

Commanding leadership, the most common style in the United States, may not represent a valid approach in many other societies. The key reason is that there are fundamental cultural differences between cultures. The personal drive, speed, decisiveness and structured individualism that form a foundation of the commanding style of leadership in the United States are not valued attributes in some other nations. . Imposing an American leadership style in these societies would cause the employees to feel disenfranchised. As a result, commitment levels would drop, and the organization would not be aligned behind the leader's vision.

There are other styles of leadership that are more important in many countries abroad. For example, in Japan consensus-building is a key characteristic of leadership style, while individuality is virtually non-existent. In Australia, a leader, first of all, is one of the mates (that is, of the group). In Finland, leadership rarely evolves unless a crisis occurs. As a result, adaptation of the commanding style outside of America could be an extremely difficult process due to differences in mentalities and historical roots of various cultures.

Non-American employees in multi-national corporations (MNCs) are accustomed to a collaborative leadership model, and would most likely react negatively to a commanding leadership style. Furthermore, companies adopt the leadership style that is most effective for the organization, and many executives outside the United States feel on balance, that the collaborative model is superior to the commanding style. A participatory leadership style has many important benefits: it engenders commitment from the organization via increased involvement; it promotes high quality decision making via discussion and debate; and it helps ensure talent development in the organization by involving many "junior" members in the decision making process.

It's possible, therefore, that in a future characterized by further globalization and by the rise of multi-national organizations, more collaborative leadership models will dominate the world scene. The key reason is that collaborative leadership is best suited for maintaining equilibrium of interests: with various voices having a contributing power to the decision-making process. Also, there are certain demographic and economic trends (in particular the rapid economic growth of China and India) that will not contribute to the American model being a top choice, since China and India have different models. Lastly, with the development of new technologies for improved communication and data sharing, co-operation and collaboration are likely to dominate the scene.

CHAPTER REFERENCES:

George, Bill. **Authentic Leadership: Rediscovering the Secrets to Creating Lasting Value.** New York: Jossey-Bass, 2003.

Goleman, Daniel, Richard Boyatzis, and Annie McKee. **Primal Leadership: Learning to Lead with Emotional Intelligence.** Boston: Harvard Business School Press, 2004.

Toffler, Barbara Lee. **Final Accounting: Ambition, Greed and the Fall of Arthur Andersen.** New York: Random House, 2003.

Ulrich, David, Jack Zenger, and Norman Smallwood. **Results-Based Leadership.** Boston: Harvard Business School Press, 1999.

ADDITIONAL READINGS:

Collins, Jim, and Porras, Jerry. **Built to Last: Successful Habits of Visionary Companies.** New York: HarperBusiness, 2002.

Pfeffer, Jeffrey. **Managing with Power: Politics and Influence in Organizations.** Boston: Harvard Business School Press, 1994.

Leadership: How to Lead, How to Live

Chapter 5

Leading at the Office

Leadership, like swimming, cannot be learned by reading about it.

- Henry Mintzberg, management thinker

In the previous chapter we explored the key elements of leadership at the broad, or strategic, level. In this chapter we look at the key skills of leadership at the narrow, or operational, level, in practice at the office or in the factory.

Leading at the Office

Leading in the limited environment of a particular business or government or nonprofit agency has special requirements. The broad leadership skills that we discussed in the previous chapter apply, but one must supplement them with operational skills. There is, for example, a considerable difference between the skills involved in the strategic and operational levels of communication.

At the strategic level, where communication primarily involves inspiring a large group of people, there is little or no feedback to the leader. A motivational speech rarely ends in a question-and-answer session; leaders address large numbers of people in one format or another and are rarely quizzed by their followers. The communication from leader to follower at the strategic level is often a speech to a large audience, a video presentation, a television program, or a pamphlet or book or other written document. None of these is much more than a one-way message.

But at the operational level, the leader must both expect and encourage two-way communication; he or she must seek feedback from his followers. There are two major reasons for this. First, the leader is trying to persuade people to take action. People generally are not persuaded if they leave a meeting with reservations about what they've heard. It's crucial for the leader to let them raise objections and to successfully address their concerns. This is a key part of the process of persuasion. Second, questions or suggestions are necessary to refine the directions or plans—so that followers can successfully carry out their tasks. In fact, the best practice for a leader is to ask followers to repeat to her what they understand their tasks to be, so she is sure they have listened carefully and fully comprehend. This is not part of

101

communication at the strategic level, but it is very important at the operational level.

This chapter is concerned with the operational level of leadership. Here the practice of leadership comes closest to management. In fact, at this level the two overlap considerably. The manager must employ operational leadership skills to be completely successful. But the manager's role also involves a considerable amount of administration, which is not the task of the leader.

We begin with a discussion of the four objectives of the operational-level leader. Then we turn to the key skills of leadership at the operational level. Next, we look at how leading differs when the "follower" is your boss or your peer rather than your subordinate. Finally, we explore a difficult but significant issue: How much tension should be welcomed (or tolerated) in a leadership team?

Key Objectives of the Operational Level Leader

An operational leader's task is made much more tractable when he or she is able to accomplish four key objectives. (See Executive Summary 5-1.) This list was generously shared with students by Gail McGovern, professor at Harvard Business School, and previously a top executive at American Telephone & Telegraph and Fidelity Investments.

While these objectives are very straight-forward, it is often difficult for leaders to step back from their daily routine and focus on these fundamental goals. The press of daily responsibilities often distracts them from this focus. However, when they do, they become significantly more effective.

EXECUTIVE SUMMARY 5-1

KEY OBJECTIVES OF THE OPERATIONAL-LEVEL LEADER

- Hire the best people.

- Learn to embrace change.

- Be resilient.

- Make every decision based on whether or not it is good for the organization.

(From: Gail McGovern, Harvard Business School.)

❖

Hire the best people: Attract, maintain and motivate the *best* people you can find. It is better to limp along with a vacancy in your staff rather than make a staffing mistake. This is hard for leaders to do because they are usually working on tight schedules, and also because a vacancy means everyone has to do more work to fill in for the missing person.

Another consideration: when you hire the wrong person, in a big organization it is usually very time-consuming and energy-intensive to get rid of him or her. There is the added psychic strain (on both sides of the equation) of having to part ways with an employee. So it's more efficient not to make a mistake, even at the cost of some delay.

It's also wise to take a risk with the job rather than with the person. Get a good person and take the risk that he or she won't do the job well rather than hire a new person you have reservations about in the belief that he or she meets the specific requirements of the job.

Leadership: How to Lead, How to Live

In looking for a key person, it's a good idea to focus less on their experience or ability to do the work than on their attitude and likely working relationship with you and others in your group. Make staffing selections as much as possible on the basis of good personal chemistry, but remember that the ultimate objective is a successful business, so you're not trying to pick people who are likely to become friends, but rather people with whom you can work well and who will add to the effectiveness of the department.

If we err, hiring a person who turns out to have a bad attitude and who becomes a focus of controversy and dislike in the group, then we will have done considerable damage. We will have set back the effectiveness of the group, and we will have missed an opportunity to carry it forward by selecting a better person for the position.

Learn to embrace change: In more and more businesses, and even in some government agencies, frequent change is common. Products change, customers change, bosses and peers change, missions change.

It sometimes seems that everything is changing. It is far better to learn to welcome change as an opportunity than to try to limit it as a harbinger of failure. The leader's role is to adjust quickly to change—to see what risks it brings and minimize them, and to see what opportunities it creates and move quickly to capitalize on them. Many people seem to hate change, but that is probably an illusion. What they hate is uncertainty about their futures, and that is something the leader can minimize if she responds quickly and correctly. So a leader should correct course quickly when significant change occurs. A leader needs to be willing to switch directions when necessary. A leader attempts to minimize danger to the firm and uncertainty to its people.

Leading at the Office

One of the most dramatic examples of the ability to correct course quickly and effectively occurred a few years ago. Microsoft's founder and chairman, Bill Gates, initially dismissed the emergence of the Internet as being of no significance to the computer industry, and indicated that Microsoft would not engage in Internet-related business. But Gates listened to Microsoft engineers who challenged his conclusion and watched the rapid development of consumer interest in the Net. He then made a major course correction for the company, a complete turnaround. Microsoft entered the Net-related business on a very large scale.

It may seem that anyone would have done this, but that's not correct. There are countless stories of business failures caused by top executives who failed to welcome change. Instead they tried to preserve existing business positions and lost out to other companies that embraced change more rapidly and effectively. For example, when personal computers first began to be linked into networks for large-scale computing, IBM's top executives refused to recognize the danger posed to mainframe computers (the large computers that IBM made and sold at a high profit). Only after the networking of personal computers using servers became so widespread and popular that the sales of mainframes were falling and IBM was losing large sums of money were new executives brought into the company to change its direction.

In the case of Digital Equipment Corporation (DEC), founder Ken Olsen refused to accept the personal computer as a rival to the midsize computers his firm manufactured, calling the personal computer a toy. So late was DEC in responding that it was not able to remain an independent company. What was DEC is now part of Hewlett-Packard Company. IBM and DEC both provide dramatic examples of the failure of top leadership to embrace change.

105

Be resilient: Leaders live in a fishbowl with everyone watching them continuously. If a leader lets personal or business setbacks cause him or her to frown, or look depressed, or grow angry, other people interpret those expressions and actions as signs of trouble in the business or in the leader's career. Rumors fly. People grow concerned, and productivity slips. To avoid these undesirable results, a leader must be resilient when faced with setbacks, keeping a smile on his face and an optimistic outlook. Mistakes should appear to roll off a leader's back. This does not mean that in private meetings with a leader's top team, he or she should paint a rosy picture even when things are going badly. But the public face must always be confident.

Make every decision based on whether or not it is good for the organization: It may seem that leaders generally make all decisions based on the good of the organization. But, just as they don't always embrace change, they don't always make decisions based on the good of the organization. Instead, they make decisions based on a variety of criteria, including what others will think of the decision. Leaders can immobilize themselves by trying to "out-think" others about decisions: How will this decision affect this group, or that? What if it doesn't work out? But decisions have to be made, and often made quickly, and without a complete understanding of what's involved or what the ultimate outcomes might be. So uncertain is the decision-making environment in business that some commentators define leadership as decision-making under uncertainty.

So the best rule is probably to make decisions that seem to promise the greatest amount of good for the organization. When colleagues see that a leader does this, they develop trust in him or her.

Key Abilities of a Leader: Operational Level

In a business, government agency, or not-for-profit organization, for a person leading a division or a department or a section, in an office or on a factory floor, there is a group of key operational skills that make it possible to achieve the four objectives discussed earlier in this chapter. These operational skills are different from the leadership skills we addressed in Chapter 4. They are more nuts-and-bolts, or down to earth, in their applicability.

Let's look at an example. A key operational skill is the ability to assess others and select the best people to hire and to assign to particular projects or tasks. If a leader can do this well, then his life becomes much easier (fewer people problems to handle) and the effectiveness of his unit is likely to improve (more productive people doing the work).

But this skill is not of much use to people in unstructured settings. For example, a political leader often gets to choose very few of his or her associates. Instead, he or she generally has to make do with those who volunteer their services.

A top-level business leader can choose some of the people who work with her closely in high-level positions, but most people are there when she arrives and remain, or are chosen by people other than herself. Therefore the more important skill at this higher level is not necessarily to pick people, but to energize them.

So the key skills we listed at the broad level of leadership were: developing a vision for the organization's future; the ability to lead by example, by inspiration, by recognizing latent ability in others; and establishing a supportive culture in which people can contribute.

Leadership: How to Lead, How to Live

In this chapter we turn to those skills that enable a leader to work successfully with a small group of people. The broader, or strategic, skills will sometimes come in handy, but it is not realistic to think of inspiring a small group of people day after day via vision or example or seeing potential or the establishment of a constructive culture—these are important elements at some infrequent intervals, or are basic, underlying conditions (like a supportive culture) that continue on a long-term basis. We look at leadership skills that pay off in the short term with small groups of people.

Ability to Energize Others

The ability to energize is critical for a leader. This skill is subtly different from a related skill of a manager: the ability to motivate the people who work for him or her. (Motivation is explored in depth in D. Quinn Mills, **Principles of Management**, Waltham, MA: MindEdge Press, 2005.) Here we explore energizing people, a key leadership skill. What is the difference?

Motivation is about using the tools a manager has available through the systems of his company to get people to do their work well. It's about using positive factors such as compensation, recognition, opportunities for promotion, and negative factors like discipline or discharge to influence people's behavior.

Energizing is a more emotional matter: It is about building commitment in an individual or team. It goes beyond inspiration (a key broad leadership skill addressed in Chapter 4) because at the operational level, inspiration must be supported by action. Many inspirational leaders don't remain with their followers to give substance to their messages. The inspirational speaker, for example, brought in by a company to

Leading at the Office

address its employees, doesn't remain to embody his message in actions. The leader who, like the motivational speaker, conveys his message and then disappears, may seem hypocritical to his audience. He is able to inspire people with his vision and eloquence, but seems unwilling to take part in the difficult work necessary to accomplish the vision.

At the operational level, leaders energize not by espousing grand ideas but by their willingness to work alongside others to bring ideas to fruition. The CEO of a hotel chain spent several days each year working at the reception desk, greeting guests entering the hotel, or sometimes working as a bell captain. The CEO of JetBlue, a low-cost airline, got a great response from employees and customers when he helped flight attendants deliver food and beverages to passengers. At his club in Palm Beach, Mara Largo, Donald Trump often has dinner with club members and visits from table to table. Getting down in the trenches with employees and customers is a way of showing that the leader respects those who do the work and receive the service at basic levels. Furthermore, good ideas can come from all ranks of an organization as well as from customers, and everyone is more willing to share ideas with leaders if they feel that leaders respect them and are willing to work with them.

Energizing a department is much easier if the leader has been able to staff the department with competent people with good attitudes. It's a valuable leadership skill to be able to quickly assess the strengths and weaknesses of others.

This ability is acquired primarily through experience—seeing the key indicators of potential success or failure in a résumé; conducting an interview in such a way that the real character and competence of the applicant emerges; using personality and aptitude tests to identify possible shortcomings. Usually, many mistakes accompany learning of this nature. But when a leader has become expert at assessing others, this skill will permit her to surround herself with the best people available and make all other aspects of leadership easier.

Ability to Communicate Clearly

It's necessary to communicate to inspire, so communication plays a key role in the strategic leadership skill of inspiration. At the operational level the key communication skill is clarity—to allow others to know what is expected of them, what they will be doing, where they fit in to the larger framework, and what will happen if something goes wrong and changes are needed. Interestingly, at the broader level of communication, clarity is much less necessary. Inspirational communication often lacks clarity—it is emotionally exciting (which is how it becomes inspiring) but it is often self-contradictory, confused, inconsistent.

If you carefully study the text of an inspirational speech, for example, you'll see that it has impact but rarely clarity. So the role of communication is very different when it's a vehicle for inspiration than when it's a vehicle for clarity.

Clear communications enable a leader to gain understanding and often agreement on a course of action. If a leader cannot get his point across clearly enough, so that its meaning and direction are well understood by the people who work with him, then he's likely to be unable to lead effectively. If one is unable to express his or her ideas clearly, one's good ideas alone are irrelevant. Although people will eventually see through style without substance, substance with no style, (or the ability to draw attention and convince others to listen and follow), will not succeed.

Although here we are stressing communications at the operational level in an organization, it is useful to recognize that even at the top of an organization clarity and simplicity in communications are critical skills. Ronald Reagan, Margaret Thatcher, and Bill Clinton are examples of political leaders whose communication skills were central to their effectiveness.

Communications are directed at a variety of people. What is the best style of communication for a diversified audience? The answer is likely to differ in different national cultures. In the U.S. people value directness; it is less valued in much of the rest of the world. In the U.S., the most effective communication style is probably to appear frank and honest, admitting mistakes and weaknesses where appropriate, and to be humorous at times. If a leader comes across as a "normal guy" and treats and speaks to others as if they were friends, then his message is more likely to be understood and accepted.

In communicating with customers and clients, leaders often find that they get more information from others by being frank rather than trying to appear too smart. It's ordinarily a disaster in the U. S. to try to outwit or "out-jargon" your audience. Instead, by taking a relaxed, humble approach a leader puts her conversation partners at ease, encouraging them to warm up to her.

When people like someone, they are more likely to accept his or her leadership. This style of communication is effective in the United States because it develops trust in the listener and thereby lowers resistance to the leader's message. (Again, these guidelines for effective small group communications do not play a significant role in communications at the strategic level, where a leader isn't usually interacting with small groups of people).

But even in the U.S. there are differences in organizations and therefore in styles of communication. For example, although openness, honesty, and humor are effective in many settings in this country, there are professional service firms (brokerage houses, investment banks, consulting companies, for example) where there is a strong premium on "polish" and formality in communications; where a leader's professional façade is much more valued; and where honesty and openness are less sought-after qualities. In these environments the most effective communication style of the leader will be more formal to fit the environment.

Some people think that the preferred communication styles for women and men differ in many cultures. This is probably not the case in the U.S. For example, a top woman executive addressed a fairly diverse audience (in terms of race, gender, nationality, type of work experience) of several hundred midlevel professionals and managers from a variety of companies. She was quickly perceived by virtually all of them as a leader. Comments about her style included:

> "She was clear, organized, and boiled some fairly complex issue into five key takeaways."

> "She has an amazing talent for being very personable to people, both those she knows and those she meets for the first time. She connects with people by making direct eye contact and she really listens to what another person has to say. You can tell that she is a very confident woman and when she speaks she wants people to take to heart what she is saying."

> "Her communication skills make her a very approachable person, which helps build trust and comprehension in those with whom she's working."

In general, the type of clarity and simplicity that this leader displayed is extremely valuable in addressing an unfamiliar audience, but also when trying to make major changes quickly in larger organizations with several layers of management. There seems little that is gender-specific about these assessments of effective communication style. The same skills would probably elicit the same favorable responses from an audience that had listened to a man.

These communication skills are critical when a leader is trying to get an entire organization to change direction. Too many executives who lack these leadership skills lose time and effectiveness trying to get an organization to change course.

Ability to Listen Effectively

Since effective two-way communication is critical at the operational level, leaders must be able to listen well. This is a much underrated skill that many leaders lack.

Effective listening requires some focus—the listener must concentrate on what he or she is hearing. Many of us don't do this well. We are much more interested in what we are going to say next, and listen only enough to pick up a cue for the topic we mean to address next. We listen to others in order to win arguments with them, rather than really considering what they are saying.

When asked a question, many people have a bad habit of giving standard answers without really hearing what has been asked; and often the standard answers are very long. Answers that are routine, too long, and not a direct response to a question can irritate an audience and cause people to lose interest in the speaker. Leaders who don't listen and who respond mechanically lose credibility.

It's important to pay attention to how people say things—to the expression on their face as they are talking, to the intonation in their voice, to their body language. Does the person seem comfortable, or is he fidgeting about as if uncomfortable (suggesting that what he is saying may not be the truth)? Does the person look away from the listener as she speaks (as if eye contact might give away that what she is saying is a deception)?

However we listen, we construct meaning out of all that we perceive—out of the words that we hear, the speaker's intonation, the expression on his or her face, the speaker's eye contact or lack thereof, the speaker's body language, and perhaps, most important of all, what is *not* said.

Advanced listeners hear clearly what the other person *doesn't* say. If the person is a potential customer and talks about the product but doesn't say anything about buying it, that alone is very significant—probably more significant than what he or she said.

A visitor came to a class at a prominent business school. She was the founder of a company; she answered questions for two hours about her business career, her family, her aspirations, her training, her leadership style. But she never referred to an episode in her life when she was a prominent leader of a student uprising against the non-democratic government of her native country. When students asked questions about it, she changed the subject.

After the class, some students complained that they had been cheated by her refusal to discuss the matter. Others pointed out that her refusal had itself been very eloquent—to them it demonstrated that she had intentionally put that phase of her life behind her and had moved on with total concentration to a new phase. To them what she had not said was as significant as what she had said. They had listened carefully to what she did not say.

Listening to what is not said is an advanced form of listening. It requires one to think, to use one's imagination, so it is a much more active form of listening than listening to another person's words. We can't tell what another person isn't saying unless we have a notion of what we might be expecting to hear.

Many students in the classroom the businesswoman visited didn't hear what she didn't say about her past political experience—because they hadn't studied her background and didn't realize she had been so involved in a famous incident. They were unable to listen to what was one of the most interesting parts of her presentation (what she chose not to say) because they weren't sufficiently prepared.

An effective listener takes time before meeting with someone or going to hear a presentation, to make a few notes about what he or she expects to hear. If those topics aren't mentioned, that represents a major learning from the session. You will see how people duck questions or ignore major topics, and you will glean much insight from that.

Some people criticize this form of listening. They say, "But if you listen to what people don't say, then you must make assumptions—that they should have been expected to say it, and if they don't, you make inferences about why. How can you know that what you surmise is correct?"

The answer is that often you cannot; but at least you have raised the question with yourself, looked for an answer about why the omission was made, and can then try to find out more about it. But the critics have a point. When you make a supposition about someone you've been listening to, it is important that it be an objective one.

A husband-and-wife business team was interviewed by a team of reporters. One of the reporters asked, "Do you two ever take work issues home?"

The wife answered, "It's important to leave work at work and keep focused on the children when at home," and the husband nodded in agreement. Then the interview went on to other topics.

Later, when the two reporters were putting together their story, one observed, "I thought it was very interesting how the two ducked the question about taking work home."

"What do you mean?" asked the other reporter. "She answered that it was important to leave work at work—here, it's in my notes."

"Yes, I heard her say that," the first reporter answered, "and I saw the husband nod in agreement. But that wasn't a direct answer to my question. I had asked if they did take work home, not if they thought they should or not. They ducked the question and I think that they probably do take work issues home—though they think they shouldn't—and probably have some problems with work issues at home."

"Aren't you making a big assumption?" asked the second reporter. "They didn't say at all that they have problems with work issues at home."

"I know," said the first reporter, "and they didn't say they didn't, which they could have said if it were true. I'd asked them exactly that."

Did the first reporter go too far with active listening (listening to what hadn't been said as well as to what had been said)? It depends in part on what the first reporter was doing. She wasn't simply fantasizing—that is, putting into someone else's words that she wanted to hear. She was instead trying to be objective about what had been said (though, of course, she could always be mistaken).

It's important for Americans to recognize that we expect communication in our society to be direct—it's part of our culture. We expect people to tell us what they really think, even if it might be embarrassing for them or us; we expect politeness, but not lack of directness. Many other cultures are different. In some cultures it's impolite to be direct; it is always necessary to "listen" to what people mean, not what they say. In the U.S. a good way to practice listening to people from other cultures is to learn to listen to what is not said as well as what is said.

Active listening involves hearing clearly what people say and recognizing what they don't say. It's a very valuable ability for a leader, and for those aspiring to leadership roles.

Ability to Earn Respect and Confidence from Others

Leaders at the operational level interact frequently with their followers. It's crucial that they earn the respect and confidence of others. It's not enough to inspire with vision. Rather, leaders must show that they have the skill to lead in the right direction and create confidence that they will be successful.

To perform effectively, people must want to succeed, not only for direct rewards, but to show respect for their leader. In a sense, all other traits of a leader are building blocks for the necessary respect. A mindset of mutual respect binds people together and enables them to perform beyond their individual capabilities.

It's a failing of many people who want to be leaders that they would rather be liked than respected. They think that if others like them, they will be able to be comfortable as part of the gang. Although all of us want to be accepted and included, the fact is that inclusion is not the fate of the leader. The leader is not part of the crowd.

What the leader wants and needs to be successful is respect—for himself or herself and for his or her role as leader. Respect is earned by the qualities of leadership—by passion, conviction, integrity, adaptability, emotional toughness and resonance, self-awareness, and humility, and by the success that comes from these qualities.

EXECUTIVE SUMMARY 5-2
FOUR KEY ABILITIES OF
OPERATIONAL-LEVEL LEADERS

- Ability to energize others
- Ability to communicate clearly
- Ability to listen effectively
- Ability to earn respect and confidence from others

———————❖———————

In the last few chapters we've offered several lists: the bases for leadership, key qualities of leadership, central skills of leadership, styles of leadership, key activities of operational-level leaders, and key abilities of operational-level leaders. These are all aspects of leadership, but they could be grouped in different ways. Some of what we call key qualities of leadership could be considered central skills of leadership. It is important, therefore, to master the elements of leadership, not the broad categories into which we group them.

Up to this point we have been discussing leadership as if it were something an individual did alone. But in many instances, leaders partner closely with others. In the next chapter we turn to that significant topic.

CHAPTER REFERENCES:

Mills, D, Quinn. **Principles of Management**. Waltham, MA: MindEdge Press, 2005.

Serven, Lawrence B. MacGregor. **The End of Office Politics as Usual: A Complete Strategy for Creating a More Productive and Profitable Organization.** New York: AMACOM, 2002.

ADDITIONAL READINGS:

Kabat-Zinn, Jon. **Wherever You Go, There You Are: Mindfulness Meditation in Everyday Life.** New York: Hyperion, 1994.

Chapter 6

Partnering with Others in Leadership

Coming together is a beginning. Keeping together is progress. Working together is success.

- Henry Ford, American industrialist

Americans tend to think of leadership as an individual thing. Our country has a single leader, our president; a company has a single leader, its CEO; and a department has a single manager. We are suspicious when there is more than one leader, fearing that there will be indecisiveness and resulting failure.

But not everyone shares this attitude. Europeans often prefer collegial leadership, in which the head of government or the CEO of a firm is one of a group of top executives who consult one another and jointly make key decisions. The Japanese, in their turn, prefer their leaders not to make decisions until they have consulted with many others in the organization, seeking a consensus on which to act.

Cooperative Leadership

Americans recognize that in some instances there may be advantages to cooperative leadership and to consensus building and so American leaders sometimes seek partners in their efforts. For example, organizations sometimes cooperate on important projects, so their leaders must work together as partners. Further, sometimes a leader recognizes that he or she has particular limitations, or blind spots, and seeks a partner who can complement his or her skills by supplying what is lacking.

In all these instances, the leader seeks a partner in leadership. Often, the partnership does not extend to everything each leader does, so it is important to clarify what it applies to and what it doesn't. (See Jon R. Katzenbach, **Teams at the Top: Unleashing the Potential of Both Teams and Individual Leaders**, Boston: Harvard Business School Press, 1997.)

The most important part of the formula for success involves finding the right partners and the right way to work with them. Finding effective partners remains significant whether the partnership is informal, as is most common, or formal, as in a business partnership or a marriage.

Finding a Partner

There are several ways to look for a partner, and the choice we make among them depends to a large degree upon our own personalities.

For example, some of us will seek people we like; others will seek people who are so like us that we can trust them to act just as we would ourselves; and others will seek people who complement us by being strong where we are weak.

What do we want in a partner? We want a person who:

- Shares our values.
- Measures success in the same way.
- Looks at our possible partnership in the same way.
- Agrees with the ethics we espouse.
- Expects what we expect from the partnership, including when and how it will end.

We are concerned about these things for two reasons.

First, so that we do not get involved with our partner in disputes that ruin the relationship or result in indecision so that we are immobilized.

Secondly, so that there are no unpleasant surprises in the future when we can't agree on important matters.

Assessing a Potential Partner

We can find out whether or not a potential partner meets these criteria by:

Spending lots of time together. Learning by experience, by little steps, by encountering problems, slowly, over as long a period as possible. Potential partners are like two ships passing in the night. At one point they come close together. But they may be going in opposite directions! Look down the road: Are there two people on parallel tracks going in the same direction, or going in opposite directions?

Negotiating a break-up in front, early on. The process of negotiation helps to define the values of the two people. What does each focus on? For example, in a for-profit company does one focus on sales, and the other on profits? This can prove to be a surprisingly wide divide between business leaders.

A growth-oriented person tries to run a company with some excess expenditures (to pay for the future growth); while a profit-oriented person just cuts costs to the bone to generate as much profit as possible. If two potential partners disagree on which is most important—growth or profit—it could signal big upcoming problems.

Talking about objectives. What kind of organization does each person want? What kind of employees? What relationship should the organization have to its employees?

Partnering with Others in Leadership

People choose partners on a variety of bases. Some of these include:

- Liking
- Complementary skills
- Experience
- Admiration
- Respect
- Common interests
- Appearance
- Family connections
- Social standing
- Wealth
- Community (ethnic, religious)

But whatever the basis, we should always take the steps recommended above to avoid incompatibility.

Probably, liking the person is the criterion most often employed. People go to meetings with a potential partner and decide whether they like the person or not. If they like him, the conversations about a partnership continue; if they don't like him, then the conversations end.

Leadership: How to Lead, How to Live

But how reliable is liking as a basis for choosing a business partner? Shouldn't complementary skills or admiration, or respect, or any of the other criteria above play a role as well, and not simply after liking?

It's tempting to think that partners in leading a business or a not-for-profit organization should:

- Carefully align their objectives.

- Agree on the way they want to achieve them.

- Make sure that they share similar values.

Without doubt, agreement on objectives is crucial to the success of any partnership. But more important than agreement on how to do things and possessing similar values may be respect for each other despite differences in methods and values.

We can explore how much liking should play a role in our search for leadership partners by examining friends as partners.

Friends as Partners

When a person sets out to find a business partner, the obvious first place to look is among his or her friends. In fact, friends often discuss starting a business together, or taking a leadership role together in some project. It would seem to make sense to partner with someone we know and trust, but what about the dynamics of working together? We already have personal ties with our friend; will business disagreements ruin our friendship? Can we make the hard decisions a project may need when a friend could be the victim?

Many people have had experience working with a friend. It can be marvelous. When there is "down time" on a project, friends can talk about common interests like sports, other friends, or nights out. Yet because the partnership is about business, a person can become extremely sensitive to a partner's behavior, for example, what time he arrives at the office, or how many long personal phone calls he makes, or how many careless mistakes he makes.

Friendship can be helpful in the early stages of a company. If the company is still growing rapidly, friends, who are typically similar in terms of background, interest, and experiences, may even speed up the business activities. But if the company is more mature, diversity may become far more important and friends may not be the best people from whom to obtain advice and get the best results.

Issues With Friends As Partners

Many people think that the risks associated with partnering with friends outweigh the benefits, regardless of the size of the venture. It becomes extremely difficult to remain objective when you are dealing with a friend. Suppose that it becomes necessary to remove your friend from the business. Stress is very much increased by friendship. A key to partnering with a friend is to somehow maintain one's objectivity and not let the friendship interfere with work decisions. In theory it seems quite simple, but it is very difficult to accomplish.

If a friend is our partner, it best to be open and honest about issues in the business or project and be careful about not being either too polite, at one extreme, or too blunt at the other, in voicing differences of opinion. Differences are best discussed openly, and a friend's criticisms should be accepted with goodwill.

The Risks of Friendship

A person had formed a company, assumed the role of CEO, and asked a friend to join the board of directors. In accepting the offer, the friend warned the CEO that some time he might have to vote against him on the board. They laughed together about the thought, as neither thought it likely to happen.

But they learned, to their regret, that sometimes ethical issues do surface when least expected. Then there was a hostile takeover attempt at the company. The CEO blocked the attempt and the stock of the company fell dramatically. The board felt that the best thing for the company was not to refuse a takeover, but to seek additional bidders for the company.

The CEO was furious, because if the company were sold, he'd lose his job; he didn't want to sell to anyone at any price. To avoid offending the CEO, his friend voted with him against other directors and against his own best judgment. This was illegal, as his responsibility was to the shareholders of the firm, not the CEO. Friendship had prevented an objective business judgment.

(See D. Quinn Mills, Stephan A. Friedrich, Hans H. Hinterhuber, and Dirk Seifert, "The Leader as Partner: A Contrast of European and American Leadership Styles," in Larraine Segil, Marshall Goldsmith, and James Belasco (eds.), **Partnering: The New Face of Leadership**, New York: AMACOM, 2003, pp. 177-86.)

Creative Tension in a Leadership Team

When we think of a partner most of us presume that the relationship will be cordial and even close. We presume that the people involved will share opinions and attitudes and largely think alike. Once, asked about a disagreement within the top executive committee of a large partnership, the CEO commented, "We don't have open disputes; we all know the business and we think alike."

But harmony between partners sometimes comes at too great a cost. There's a danger in organizations that a leader will assemble a group of close associates with whom he or she is comfortable, and that they will become subject to a destructive process of "group think." The group will not challenge the leader in his or her thinking, but will instead praise the leader continually for all he or she says and proposes to do.

Where is the danger for the organization in this scenario? Objectivity, honesty, and creativity will disappear from the group in favor of subjectivity, dissembling, and a continuing preference for the status quo. The organization will slowly become prey to more objective and imaginative rivals.

The history of business and government is full of this pattern of group think. The only way to avoid it is for the leader to actively encourage open discussion of differing views. The leader must draw into his or her inner circle of confidantes people who have divergent views and reward a degree of dissent with the dominant thinking in the group. Where there is dissent and disagreement, there will necessarily be some tension. If one leads properly, the tension will be creative and constructive. If one leads improperly, it will be divisive and destructive.

Because of the danger of divisiveness, there is no role for creative tension in an administrative team. The efficiency with which a leader manages his team, implementing the policies of the organization as determined by senior administrators, would be compromised by creativity or tension or both. But in the leadership team of any organization there is a role for different opinions, controversies, and the tension among individuals that is likely to accompany differences. The issue is: How much tension is creative, and when does creativity go too far and dysfunctional conflict emerge?

Many people find it difficult to distinguish between constructive dissent and destructive conflict within a group of people. When they observe disagreement within a top leadership team, they view it as counterproductive and accuse the leader of allowing subordinates to cross a line between challenging and disrespecting. They believe that a dynamic that involves disagreement at best ensures that the organization functions at a suboptimal level, and at worst is a recipe for eventual disaster. Some people believe that no company can achieve success without agreement among its senior executives.

When top leaders have very different styles and clearly disagree about important issues, then employees often try to align themselves with one or the other. This can create a dangerous division within the organization. People who are concerned about this dynamic will add that it is healthy for leaders to disagree with colleagues, but insist that the way in which they disagree can make or break relationships and can destroy the cohesion of the organization generally.

How can we reconcile the need for divergence of opinion with the need for cooperation and respect?

One key is that open discussion should be limited to the leadership team, and the team should always present a common front to the broader organization and to outsiders. Examples are instructive:

"I ran a company for nearly three years with a co-CEO. In our offices, with the doors closed, we argued quite often but we would always try to present a united front to our employees."

"I was the operations officer on a destroyer in the Persian Gulf and I frequently disagreed vehemently with the captain of the ship, its executive officer, and fellow department heads. One thing I learned was never to openly engage in arguments with other senior officers in front of subordinates...I have witnessed such arguments between senior officers and seen the damage it does to the morale of enlisted personnel. Lowering morale in this way generally leads to difficulties down the road when sailors feel they are getting mixed messages from their leaders."

Another important way to avoid disaster is for the top leaders to agree to disagree. Where the situation permits, the leaders do not proceed to an action until they reach a unanimous decision. Then, even though one leader may totally disagree with another's plan, she will still support the effort if that is the decision that has been reached. Such a resolution implies a great respect for others who have divergent points of view and approach implementation differently.

The third contributor to success is that even though two leaders have different approaches, disagree often, and sometimes even dislike each other, they respect each other. It is possible to respect someone we don't particularly like. After all, in working with another person, we are not marrying him or her—it's a business relationship. People who complement each other—who have different strengths—can respect each other's capabilities. An organization may need the talents of both for success. When success comes from their joint efforts, they are able to respect one another.

Sometimes partners discuss how to do something. Most of us presume that they are trying to agree on a method, and when they reach agreement, they decide who will lead the effort and whichever one it is, that person will do what they've agreed. In effect, either one could lead the effort and both would do it the same way.

But this is too limited a view. In fact, people often have different styles and convictions. When actually leading an initiative, one partner would do one thing and the other another thing. The partners disagree about how to do something and cannot resolve the disagreement. They discuss it and fully understand each other's position, but still don't agree. Then they decide who will lead the effort, and that whoever does it will use the method she thinks right. The other leader, who wouldn't do it that way at all, accepts the alternative approach with goodwill because he has confidence that his partner, using her own method, will succeed. It requires a lot of self-discipline for one partner to let the other handle a major matter in a way that the first partner disagrees with; and he or she is likely to do that only because of great respect for the other partner. In this sort of relationship there is a tension that never fully disappears, for it is grounded too deeply in the divergent experiences and attitudes of the two people.

Tension of this nature we often take to be destructive, but it can be constructive and creative. Creative tension is about divergent approaches and new ideas. It's meant to bracket a problem with different perspectives and different alternatives for action. It is not criticism for criticism's sake. Instead, creative tension involves an environment in which people are able to express and push for their ideas in order to achieve the best possible final outcome. A certain amount of tension results, but it is of a creative, constructive type.

Controversies That Can Ruin a Partnership Among Leaders

We saw above that disagreements among partners can be either destructive or constructive, depending on several things. In this section we look at the kind of controversies that can ruin a partnership.

What are the key controversies that paralyze action among partners in leadership?

1. Long-Term Visionary Versus Short-Term Opportunist

A partnership must have a long-term vision of what it seeks to accomplish; but this doesn't imply a necessary blindness to short-term opportunities. Nor does seeking to grasp a short-term opportunity imply that a longer-term vision has to be sacrificed. But if partners in leadership get into a dispute about whether or not to take a short-term opportunity because of its alleged lack of fit with the long-term vision, then action can be stymied.

2. Inclusive Versus Exclusive Attitudes

Some partners argue for wide inclusion of others in an effort by the organization, including all those likely to be affected by an initiative. Others feel that for action to be prompt, it's necessary to limit the degree of inclusion. The partner who supports inclusion is likely to believe that exclusion implies elitism and risks obtaining necessary support in the broader organization. The partner who supports exclusion is likely to believe that inclusiveness so dilutes those who hold the vision that action drifts about aimlessly. Unable to decide whom to include and whom to exclude, the partners argue to no good end.

3. Preference for Exploratory Versus Immediate Action

Addressing a major initiative, some partners will want to move slowly, exploring the vision and determining how to proceed; others will want to adopt definite goals and move aggressively toward them. The partner who wants to move slowly is likely to feel that aggressive action is insensitive to concerns about unintended negative consequences of action—that is, insensitive to possible bad results. But the partner who wants to move aggressively is likely to feel that going slowly will cause the organization to miss its opportunity. An inability to agree may leave the organization immobilized by indecision.

4. Preference for Collaborative Versus Competitive Action

If both partners support a course of action and agree that each should be part of the organization in implementation, should there be only collaboration between the two groups, or should they compete with each other? The argument for competition is that it's a major motivator for people; the argument for collaboration is that by cooperating the two groups can share learning and increase the effectiveness of both. It's often hoped that groups in an organization can both compete and collaborate at the same time, but this assumes a great deal about human nature. People who are competing with each other are not likely to share with their opponents the ideas that they hope will provide victory. So usually it's either collaboration or competition, and if the partners can't decide, again the organization is immobilized.

5. Self-Interest Versus Wider Interests

Certain issues are more likely to arise among partners in leadership in a not-for-profit organization than in a for-profit business. This is because not-for-profit leaders generally have missions promoting the public welfare and are often deeply concerned with ethical issues. So when a not-for-profit considers an important project, conflict-of-interest questions may arise: If there is self-gain, is the morality of the project thereby compromised?

For example, suppose that for-profit companies are going to cooperate with a not-for-profit organization in a project. The objective of the project is the public good; but the for-profit firms hope for some additional business as a result of the project (for example, as a result of advertising about their involvement in the project). Does that undermine the ethics of the project? One partner in leadership may say yes; the other, no. Here is yet another point at which an initiative could be stalled because of a disagreement among partners.

It is not a matter of simply determining right or wrong. Both partners can have strongly held beliefs and both can (correctly) feel that they are pursuing an ethical or moral course.

Each of these areas of controversy has the potential to stall effective action in a partnership. It is easy to imagine how different partners might have varying opinions on such issues and how long and contentious the arguments about them could be.

Yet these areas of controversy can sometimes be overcome; they appear to be insurmountable, but aren't, if the partners involved can reach a balance on them. Hence, partnering among leaders is about mutual respect and the ability to accommodate and balance different opinions and attitudes. (See D. Quinn Mills and Ian Somerville, "Leading in a Leaderless World," *Leader to Leader*, 13 (Summer, 1999), pp. 30-38.)

CHAPTER REFERENCES:

Katzenbach, Jon R. **Teams at the Top: Unleashing the Potential of Both Teams and Individual Leaders.** Boston: Harvard Business School Press, 1997.

Segil, Larraine and Marshall Goldsmith, James Belasco (eds.). **Partnering: The New Face of Leadership.** New York: AMACOM, 2003.

ADDITIONAL READINGS:

Gergen, David. **Eyewitness to Power.** New York: Simon & Schuster, 2001.

Gerstner, Louis. **Who Says Elephants Can't Dance?** New York: HarperBusiness, 2002.

Leadership: How to Lead, How to Live

PART III

BUILDING OUR CAREERS TO LEADERSHIP POSITIONS

Leadership: How to Lead, How to Live

Chapter 7

Career Paths to Leadership

The secret of a leader lies in the tests he has faced over the whole course of his life and the habit of action he develops in meeting those tests.

- Gail Sheehy, American journalist

Leadership: How to Lead, How to Live

People who become top leaders generally share two characteristics:

- They set a few clear priorities and stick to them. They know what is most important to them, and they forgo other things as distractions. To other people this may suggest that leaders sacrifice things for which they haven't time or attention; but for the achievers, giving up something in order to pursue a higher priority item is not a sacrifice at all.

- Their lives are very structured, in order to be sure that the things that need to get done do, in fact, get done. Since few people give sole priority to their work, this means that time is allocated on a deliberate basis not only to work but to family and other priorities. Sometimes structuring reaches dramatic proportions – as, for example, when a person sets a certain time each day to see his or her spouse.

To other people this much structuring may suggest spontaneity is gone, and life may not seem worth living. To the achievers, there is often some room for some spontaneity within the overall structure.

Career Paths to Leadership

People customarily try to reach positions of broad leadership in their organizations through the career paths they choose. There are as many career paths as there are people, but we can identify some key patterns of careers.

Here are a few illustrative examples of differing career paths.

Bill's Progress Up the Promotion Ladder

Bill began his career by taking a sales job in a large company. He was very personable and enjoyed other people, often strong characteristics for a salesperson. Over the years he worked hard, managed his relationship with his bosses and peers well, and was steadily promoted. He came to the attention of top management and was selected for training. Upon completing the training programs he was given wider responsibilities. Ultimately, he was given responsibility for a division of the company and for the first time had responsibility for the bottom-line profit or loss (until then he had always headed what is called a cost center, a department with an expense budget that he was required to follow.)

With responsibility for profit or loss, Bill was in charge of sales of his division's products that were revenue producing, as well as budgeted costs. He tried to maximize sales and keep costs to budgeted levels, thereby generating profits. When he demonstrated that he could successfully generate profits from his division, he was advanced to the position of chief operating officer (COO) of the company.

From that position he observed the company's chief executive officer closely, learning how she led the company. When she retired, the board of directors selected him as CEO.

143

Many of us think of Bill's progress up the promotion ladder in a single company as what a career is. But there are many other paths to the top.

Jorge's Move to a New Company

Jorge had been at a large company for ten years, climbing the management ladder, envisaging a career like Bill's in his mind. Then he hit a wall. He realized that for a number of reasons, he wasn't going to go any higher. He began to look around for something else. A rapidly growing company was looking for a top executive. He studied the company and then obtained an interview. He was offered the job. He hesitated momentarily before accepting it. He'd had his heart set on a high position in his current firm—it was a larger firm, better established, and he knew it well. Shifting to a different firm would mean that he had to spend lots of time and effort learning about the new company, getting to know the many people in and outside the firm who were crucial to its success in the future, and taking a risk that he wouldn't succeed at the new firm, or that the firm itself might not succeed.

But he believed in the mission of the new company; he saw the risks as exciting challenges; and he saw above him the path open to the CEO's job if he performed well. He took the job and five years later was made CEO of the firm.

Gayle's Move Up, Across, and Up Again

We usually think of a career path as ascending a ladder in an organization, but that is too narrow a view. In most large organizations there are a number of different departments and divisions. At lower levels of management there are dozens of positions in various departments and divisions, although at the CEO level there is only one position. Most people who are trying to make their way to more responsible positions in a large organization are reluctant to ever take a step down or even to make a lateral move; they want every job change to be a step up the promotion ladder.

But often this attitude is a mistake. A very good person can get stuck in a particular position and not get promoted for a variety of reasons. For example, there may be a person in the job ahead of him or her who is not going to be promoted, but is going to remain there indefinitely. Then the promotion path is blocked, no matter how well the person at the lower level performs. Or a person may be so valuable to her department, that the department head refuses to recommend her for promotion, trying to retain her services in the department. This shouldn't happen—it isn't ethical and most companies discourage it strongly—but it does sometimes occur.

What is a person to do who finds the path to promotion blocked in these ways?

She might do what Gayle did. When she graduated from college, Gayle was hired by a large firm to work in the information technology area. She was an individual contributor, but was given some assignments to manage project teams and discovered that she liked to manage. However, the department in which she was working was not growing, and her path up the promotion ladder was blocked. So she looked for a low-level management job, and found one in another department. There, over the next few years she was promoted twice, only find the path up blocked again by other people.

So after two years in the same job, and with no prospect of near-term promotion, she looked for a position at the same level in another department, and found one. She took a lateral transfer. But in her new department there were promotion opportunities and soon she was again climbing the corporate ladder. She formulated a rule for herself: that she wouldn't remain in a single job for more than two years. If there was no promotion likely, she'd move laterally. In one instance, she actually took a downgrade in moving to another department. But that department was growing rapidly and in six months she was promoted to what had been her previous level, and then soon after, another promotion put her higher than where she'd been before her lateral move.

With each shift of departments she was also getting valuable experience in different aspects of the business. With another lateral move, she found herself on the path to the top of the firm.

Walter's Here-and-There Career

An increasingly common career path begins in a professional services firm and then jumps to a different type of firm. But when the jump occurs it is at a high level. In effect, then, the jumper has skipped years of what the military calls "time in grade" waiting for promotions. Rather than work his or her way up in an organization, the jumper starts elsewhere and then jumps to the organization he wants to be in—not at the bottom, but near the top.

Walter left college and took a job in a bank. He spent four years there, and then went to business school. Upon graduating with his MBA, he took a job in a large consulting company. There Walter spent ten years, traveling to client firms in the United States and abroad, learning about several industries and the companies in them in great detail in his role as a consultant. He developed a special attachment to the CEO of a major manufacturing company. Walter developed its strategic plan and spent many days with the CEO working out the plan's implementation.

When the CEO wanted to fill the second-ranking position in the company, the position of chief operating officer, he turned to Walter. Without regret, for this is what he'd been waiting for, Walter left the consulting company and signed on with the manufacturing firm. In his COO job, Walter got firsthand experience in every aspect of the firm's businesses and became well known to the members of the firm's board of directors. Five years after Walter joined the firm, the CEO retired and Walter was chosen by the board to be the new CEO.

Andy's Jump to the Big Time

From an early age Andy had wanted to run a large company. But when he graduated from business school, he took a job not in an operating company with a career ladder to climb, but in a consulting company. He learned a lot about consulting, but he wasn't getting close to his desire to run a large company. But no big company seemed interested in him.

Then he got a call from some friends about a small company they'd started that needed a new CEO. He looked it over, and decided that at least in the new company, little though it was, he could learn something about actually managing a company rather than merely giving advice to the managers. So Andy took the job.

Soon he discovered that the company was on the brink of failure. Andy worked very hard and brought it out of the danger zone. Then he was able to help it grow and become successful.

A large company noticed Andy's little firm and offered to buy it. The price was so good that his board of directors wanted to accept the offer and Andy had no alternative but to see the firm sold.

To his surprise, the buyer wanted him to stay and run the firm, but as their employee. He agreed. He did so well with his small division of the big firm, that his new bosses bought other companies to add to his division. It grew rapidly until it was the largest and most profitable division of the firm. At that point, he was offered the CEO's job in the large company. From the tiny start-up, Andy had launched himself on the path to a CEO's chair in a big company.

Steve Builds Himself a Company

Steve graduated from college as an engineer. He got a job with a rapidly growing software firm and learned a lot. Then he returned to business school and got an MBA. All the time he was there he looked for an idea for a new business, and looked for people who could help him with it. When he graduated he already had a business plan and a few people ready to become his employees. He bought some computers, set them up in the small living room and kitchen of his apartment, crowded himself into its single bedroom to live, abandoned his private life, and went to work day and night.

Soon Steve was able to raise some money and move his employees out of his apartment into a small set of rooms in an office building. They worked hard, raised more money from investors, and finally began to bring in large clients. He took the company public, expanded it further, and found himself CEO of a rapidly growing company.

Simin's Trans-Pacific Adventure

Shao Simin was born in China and came to the United States as a refugee when a student protest against the government in which she participated became violent and Simin had to flee the country.

In America she found sponsors who helped her finish college. She met some people who were impressed with her leadership potential as it had been demonstrated in China. She married an American businessman, became a U.S. citizen, and soon they started their own firm. Her husband was most interested in working with investors and customers; she in running the company's internal operations. There Simin found a rewarding career and opportunity to exercise her interest in management.

We've looked at the careers of several people as they followed different paths to positions offering the opportunity to exercise significant leadership. Below we summarize the paths these people took:

1) *Within a single company*
   Climbing the promotion ladder (Bill)
   Moving laterally while climbing the ladder (Gayle)

2) *Moving among companies*
   In an industry, moving among competitors (Walter)
   Moving from industry to industry - for example, from a consulting company to a manufacturing, transportation, or retail company (Andy)

3) *Forming a new company* (Steve, Simin)

How to Get Started on a Path to Greatness

An important consideration in building a career is that most of us start near the bottom of the promotion ladder. Many of us have talent as leaders, or are willing to develop it, but the tasks we encounter in our early jobs don't involve much leadership. We are often expected to serve our time in low-level positions, waiting in line for promotion up the career ladder. But many of us are impatient. Some of us think we'd make a terrible junior employee in a large company; yet we are convinced that some day we'd do very well filling a high-level leadership position in the firm. If that's the case, what is the best way to achieve such an objective?

One way to plan a career is to seek environments in which we'd thrive at each stage of our careers, moving from one job to another as we mature.

Often, successful leaders toward the end of their careers advise us that the best path to success is to follow our hearts. We should look for something to do in which we have great interest, or for which we have a great passion, and do that, because we're more likely to be able to commit the time and energy over the long period necessary to climb to broad leadership positions.

What does it mean to follow our hearts? It doesn't mean to follow a fantasy, for example, to try to be movie stars or rock stars, or president of our country (although some of us might do each of these things). But it does mean finding something that really intrigues us and that we will love doing. For example, a young person who's very excited about putting new TV shows on the air might seek a job in the media business.

But we have to do more than identify what excites us. Each of us should identify our talents, skills, and gifts—the things we're good at, and our passions, what we're especially interested in—and try to combine them into something that feels exactly right for us. If we can find a way to combine these two aspects (skills and passion) of our personalities into a career, and thereby follow our hearts, then we're likely to be much happier and more successful.

But it's surprisingly difficult to follow our hearts. Often the most difficult person to be honest with is oneself. Many of us claim to live our lives in ways that seem to those who know us very different from the way we actually live them, and this inconsistency is likely to increase over time until it becomes a form of denial. When we encounter someone who appears to be inconsistent in this regard, we often presume that the person knows what he is really like, but pretends to be something else—that is, that he's a hypocrite. But often, the person actually believes that he is different than he is. This is a common human trait, but not a good one. Some of us have done self-evaluation exercises and others will be doing them either at a college or with a counselor in a company.

Often, when we do these exercises, we think we're being honest with ourselves, only to retake the same exercises a year or so later and discover that a lot of what we'd said before wasn't entirely true; instead, it was what we thought we should want. In the time that has passed, we've grown more certain of our own interests and better able to identify our desires.

It's difficult to take a serious look at ourselves. What's even more difficult is that we need to keep doing it—over and over again—as necessary during our careers. In general, we will not truly come into our own as potential leaders until we find something that we are passionate about and are able to pursue in a supportive environment. "Following your heart" refers to your long-term goal and it is up to each of us to determine how to get there.

Following the Herd

In choosing a career many of us are likely to be strongly influenced by what our friends and acquaintances are doing. If most people we know are thinking of working in the local manufacturing company and trying to climb a career ladder, others find that a natural thing to do. If most are thinking of going into consulting; others will also. If most are fascinated by the apparent opportunities in a new technology, so will others. But following the herd is often not the best choice. Instead, we should be looking for something—an industry, a field of endeavor, a mission—that we really care about.

It's only when the herd is doing what we also really want to do, something we have a passion for, that we should follow the herd. But then, it's fine—not because the herd is doing it, but because it's something we really want to do.

Getting Ahead in Our Careers

Here are three ways that we can move ahead in our careers:

- Get a sponsor or two (not just a mentor);
- Cultivate the perceptions you want others to have of you (being seen as decisive, for example);
- Be flexible about your assignments;
- Have balance in your life so you don't burn out.

We will succeed in getting ahead if we put in the time to develop our career.

Get a sponsor or two. Most people need not only a mentor, but a sponsor – someone who not only shows them the ropes and advises them, but someone who pushes strongly for them with higher management. For most of us, decisions about promotions, new assignments and compensation are all made without us present by higher-level management. Who is there to push for us? Mentors often don't do that – they are not our champions but are instead our advisors. So we need a sponsor or a champion to go to bat for us.

Cultivate the right perceptions. Perceptions that other people have of you are critical. Try to determine what those perceptions are and make them as positive as possible. At each stage of your career, try to identify three adjectives that you want other people to use to describe you, and reinforce perceptions that are reflected in those adjectives. The adjectives should always be appropriate in three ways: they should fit what you are or what you can become; they should be things that are important and valuable to the company; and they should fit your stage of career.

Suppose, for example, you have been in a staff position in which you wanted to appear analytic, careful, and imaginative.

Suddenly, you are assigned to a line job in a factory, supervising production employees. Now you want to appear strong, decisive, and results-oriented.

How does a person make the change from one set of preferred adjectives to another? First, try to actually be like the new requirements.

Second, take opportunities to stress the new adjectives because other people may not notice the change in us unless we call it to their attention. We need not only to act decisive, but to tell other people that we are decisive. "I made a decision about this; I made a decision about that." There is a bit of self-promotion in this that may not appear seemly, but in a big organization other people are pre-occupied and busy and it may be necessary to point things out to them.

However, we might question the advisability of guiding a career based on how others might perceive us. This type of strategy seems to be without a strong, personal foundation, but rather rooted in an ever-changing world of other people's opinions. At the end of the day, it's impossible to control how others view us, since there are so many variables we can't control, for example, I might remind another person of someone else and be unable to shake an already established negative opinion.

So it's risky for a person to base a career primarily on an effort to control his or her image. Some people might think it idealistic, but prefer to be their selves and let the chips fall where they may. They might think, "If people don't like me, so what? As long as I'm comfortable with myself, does it really matter?

Be flexible. An area which we think is a good assignment may turn out not to be. When alternatives come up, consider them carefully, and be prepared to move, assignments, departments, bosses, locations, and even, sometimes, companies. The economy changes direction much faster than it used to. What seem to be reliable market directions can collapse very quickly. So we need to keep our eyes open and shift when necessary.

We are shaped by our experiences and our environment, and we can all change. We can do it by changing ourselves to fit a new environment to which we are assigned by others; or we can seek out a new environment as a way of changing ourselves.

We all make mistakes; we can always turn around our errors, even if it takes some effort.

Have balance in my life so that I don't burn out. Most of us need variety in our lives to keep fresh. If we work a lot of the time and don't get away from work, we are likely to get tired and lose our vitality. This is how people burn-out. It's very important to take actions to avoid burn-out.

Five Patterns of Extraordinary Careers

James M. Citrin and Richard A. Smith in their book **The Five Patterns of Extraordinary Careers** (New York: Random House, 2003.) outline a number of key actions we can take to position ourselves for an extraordinary career.

Understand the value we can contribute to the organization. It's nice when our boss and our peers will identify us as outstanding performers who deserve help up the career ladder, but it's often not so simple. Instead, we may have to point out to others the importance of what we specifically contribute to the organization. To do that effectively, we have to clearly understand our value.

This doesn't mean that we become braggarts; but it does mean that we quietly help others understand where we are making important contributions.

Get carried to the top. Many of us imagine a dog-eat-dog world in which we bite and claw our way to the top. This is sometimes the case, but often the opposite occurs—others recognize our value and carry us along to higher positions.

Get the job we want without the (supposedly) necessary experience. It's a difficult paradox that often we can't get the job we want because we lack the experience; and we can't get the experience because we don't have the job. This is a major barrier to many people on the route to obtaining a high position in an organization.

There are several ways to break through the logjam. One is to build a personal reputation so that when a key job is empty and there is no candidate with strong experience seeking it, we become the choice to fill the position.

Often a company will fit the job to the person rather than the other way around. Another way is to assemble in bits and pieces some of the experience called for by the position.

Do more than is expected. Don't stop at the job requirements. Let others see that we're qualified for greater responsibility.

In climbing a promotions ladder, we should expect to go from being an individual contributor to being a supervisor, to being a manager, and finally to being a top executive. We can exercise leadership at any level, but as we advance, the proportion of our effort that is leadership increases considerably from individual performer to supervisor to manager to top executive.

Look to the long term, not just the next career step. We should follow our hearts about what we really want to do, and let every position we take become a stepping stone to our long-term goals, even if our path is a bit wandering rather than simple and direct.

Career Choice: Choose the Area in Which We Have the Best Skills, or the One We Like Best?

People often choose careers for the wrong reasons: It's the first job we're offered; it's the best-paying job we can get at the moment; it's convenient to where we live; it gives us a lot of time off. These are attractive features of a job offer at the outset, but rarely do these features last; or if they last, often they lose their attractiveness.

For example, taking the first job offered may keep us from more attractive ones that come along later; what is a high-paying job at the outset may not have much opportunity for progress up a pay scale; we relocate our residence, and discover that no longer is the job's location attractive; we decide at some point that time off is less important, and opportunities for advancement become more important, but the job we took doesn't offer that.

There are several good reasons for selecting a particular job:

- It's something we're very interested in or passionate about.

- It's something we're very good at.

- It has a lot of potential for personal advancement.

It is ideal when we can find a position that combines all three reasons. Then we have a job that involves work in which we're very interested, even passionate about; it's something we're very good at; and it offers many opportunities for advancement in position, responsibility, and compensation.

Problems arise, however, when the three considerations don't mesh. For example, what should you do if you're very good at something you don't care much about; and you care a lot about something you're not very good at?

Leadership: How to Lead, How to Live

The choice of what to do and how to pursue our own development becomes more difficult because there is a great advantage to be very good at one thing, rather than okay at several things. We have a group of talents, some of which are more developed than others. Consider A, B, and C talents; we're best at A, moderate at B, and poor at C. We think that developing ourselves means to improve on C; but our contribution may instead be maximized by doing better at A.

The real contribution in a large organization is made by people who are very good at some things, rather than equally good at a number of things. A large organization has specialists in each. Therefore, we need to develop our own competitive advantage by improving what we are best at, not by trying to be good at everything. There is, of course, an exception. Sometimes a person is so poor on C—for example, interpersonal skills—that the lack thereof gets in the way of his contribution on A. This does need fixing, but that's not so much development as remediation.

Which should you choose: something you care a lot about or something you are very good at? And what if the thing you care about lacks advancement potential, and the thing you're good at also lacks advancement potential?

How you make a choice in this difficult situation is likely to be a defining moment for your career.

Career Choices

We saw earlier that Bill chose a job he was very good at. And he wasn't dissatisfied, because in many cases if we're good at something, at least we enjoy it, even though it may not be something we care deeply about. In addition, there's much less risk of failure in choosing something we're good at than in choosing something we care about, but have to learn how to do well. We might not ever be able to learn to do it well.

But is Bill's choice the one we'd make for ourselves? Many of us have limited years of work experience and don't know what we might really be good at in a specific job function or industry. And even if we believe we're good at something today, it might not be sustainable and viable as time wears on.

Some people advise us to avoid what they consider the trap of choosing a job because we think we're good at it. Instead, they advise us to go after the thing we're passionate about. But this can be hazardous if we have a curiosity to try new things, and the curiosity turns out not to be a true passion. Jumping from interest to interest can have some negative career impacts; some potential employers look warily at "job hoppers."

Also, we can be passionate about something for which we have no real aptitude. For example, we may care passionately about professional basketball, but (unfortunately) have absolutely no capability to be an NBA star! However, within our range of competence, if we choose a job or company we're passionate about, it's likely that we will be inspired to fully master the challenges we confront and achieve a successful career. Otherwise, we may end up going through the motions in our careers, which can be potentially dangerous to both ourselves and the organization for which we work.

So we must each look for a combination of the three factors that suits us. For the most fortunate of us, the three factors coincide: What we care most about is what we're best at, and this overlapping offers us a career with great potential for advancement and financial reward. For some of us, at least two of the three coincide: What we care most about is what we're best at, even though our long-term potential for advancement is limited. Careers in the helping professions (like health care and education) often are like this. Or it may be that we are good at something that offers career advancement, for example, information technology.

Finally, it may be that we care a lot about something that has great potential, and though we don't know how to do it yet, we're prepared to put in the time and effort to learn, and take the risk that we might never be very good at it.

The most difficult situation is faced by those for whom there is no coincidence among the three factors, so they must choose among them: that is, decide to enter a profession they care a great deal about, or one they are good at, or yet another that has better potential than the others.

The decision is very difficult because the opportunity with the greatest potential is one we don't care much about and aren't very good at; the opportunity we care most about, we're not very good at and lacks advancement potential; and finally, the position for which we're best suited by competence, is one we don't care about and that has little advancement potential.

In this environment, we define ourselves by the choice we make. One person will choose ambition above caring and skill; another will choose skill and the security that goes with it; and a third will choose his or her passion, going all out and hoping for the best. For the third group perhaps the best advice is to do what you love and try to find someone to pay you to do it.

We should each ask ourselves, "What situation am I in? How should I make my career choice?"

Finding Our Career "Sweet Spots"

We increase the likelihood of advancing in our careers if we can bring together what motivates us (our passion) and what we are good at (our capabilities). We call this intersection a person's career "sweet spot." Unfortunately, it may prove difficult to find our sweet spot because we may not be good at something that we feel passionate about. There are areas that some of us may have passion for—art, music, dance, sports, food, entertaining—but it is rare for a person to develop a full-fledged career in these areas.

One way to help bring the two together is to try to obtain the skills and capabilities necessary to succeed in something that we're passionate about. Sometimes we rush to find a job that is in our sweet spot, but cannot, because we haven't the skills to match to our passion. So it's better to invest the time in acquiring the skills necessary to do well in something we care about, and then look for the perfect match. Many people go into consulting early in their careers for this very reason. In consulting a person can pick up a wide variety of skills, and develop abilities and personal contacts that will help one get a position in a particular industry.

Another partial step that may be possible for many of us is to find an element of our jobs that we are passionate about. For example, a manager in a health services firm might not be particularly passionate about the administrative work, travel, and internal politics, but he might have considerable passion about saving lives with the company's medical devices.

In some instances it may take a long time to find a career that matches our sweet spots. But as long as we keep this goal in mind as we pursue our career paths, many of us will eventually come across a job that comes close to our own personal special intersection of passion and competence.

For some of us there will never be an intersection of passion and competence in the work environment. But all is not lost.

First, many people take jobs that have no relation to their passions. They expect to dislike the job immensely, but instead end up loving the job. Why? Because of the people and the teams they work with, because of the positive culture of the firm, and because of the energy of the place. While they may not be working in an industry whose products they love, they've found passion for their jobs nonetheless.

For many of us, finding this sort of passion at work, regardless of the industry, might be a more plausible way to embrace our sweet spots. In this situation, the sweet spot is a working environment that motivates us.

For example, a young man has spent a bit of time working in a capital markets role. Although he doesn't love the hours or sometimes the companies he works with, he does enjoy the excitement of doing a deal. The fun he has—and the enjoyment he receives from the environment—compensate him for the parts of the job that he doesn't enjoy as much.

Exploring Career "Sweet Spots"

Sometimes we are able to use summer internships to experience the working environment of a company before making a decision about whether or not we would enjoy working there. Without working in a company, it is difficult to gauge the type of working environment that exists.

Second, in some cases the sweet spot is not sweet at all, but more sour. For example, a young woman who had always been passionate about music took a summer between semesters in college as an opportunity to explore the music business in Los Angeles. She hoped that she might be one of those rare persons for whom passion and talent meshed at an early stage of life.

But as it turned out, the business of music was not for her. She found it frustrating to work in an industry in which she found it difficult to be successful, while still remaining passionate about it. Although it's easy to imagine things that would seem to be fun to do, for some of us it's quite healthy to distance career from true passion. Music will always be among this young woman's favorite things; she just couldn't bear to do it for a living. She is now searching for another field in which she can combine her passion with her abilities without experiencing frustration in trying to achieve results.

Shifting Our Career Paths

Jorge hit a wall at his first employer and was fed up with bureaucracy. He then moved to a new company because he believed in its mission and thought that he could one day achieve his goal of becoming CEO at the company. Like Jorge, at some point in our careers some of us will "hit a wall" and want to move to a different company.

It is not easy to determine when we should make a significant shift in our career paths. People who have been successful can often relate how and why they made a significant shift that led to greatness, and suggest that had they not made the change, their careers would have stagnated.

The best guide to developing our careers may be our own internal sense of fit or satisfaction when we are at a particular point in our careers. There is a danger of ignoring this feeling because of other considerations; we may not be completely ready to confront the uncertainty of a shift.

The old saw, "the harder I work, the luckier I get," explains why opportunities emerge for some people and not others. But luck also plays a role. We should not spend our lives planning our entire careers or worrying about our rise to the top of an industry. To do so would be to risk taking ourselves too seriously. Twenty years from now, those of us who are happily working in fulfilling jobs can look back on our successful careers without regret and can congratulate our colleagues—who may be CEOs of Fortune 500 firms or top government leaders—on their good fortune.

Many successful people have not followed a well-defined career plan. Instead, they have been ready to take advantage of opportunities that have presented themselves along the way. Inevitably, we will face unexpected forks in the road, where we will be forced to make life-altering decisions. We can hope that through our experiences in school and work, we will know our abilities and our passions well enough to make the choices that will allow us to optimize our abilities and find the maximum level of fulfillment.

Suppose each of us wants to climb the corporate ladder to a position of influence. One imaginative way to approach the challenge is to try to make our own resumes as much like that of the people who are running the company as we can. So we might look at their resumes—usually readily available on company websites or in annual reports. Commonly such resumes show experience in many of the business units of the company. So try to get experience in as many business units as we can—even by lateral transfers. Our objective is to learn enough about the business as a whole to be able to manage its profit and loss statement. In general, it's important to get some experience in a revenue-generating role if we want to rise to the top of management because a very important goal of a business is to generate revenues. It's crucial to have a hands-on understanding of how the company makes money.

Success is often not about making plans, but about how we react to unexpected opportunities. Leadership opportunities present themselves in many settings. We are about to examine several of the most important ones, so that we can begin to decide where we would be most comfortable looking for a fulfilling leadership career.

Leadership: How to Lead, How to Live

CHAPTER REFERENCES:

Citrin, James M. and Richard A. Smith. **The Five Patterns of Extraordinary Careers**. New York: Random House, 2003.

ADDITIONAL READINGS:

Bell, Ella L. J. E. and Stella M. Nkomo. **Our Separate Ways: Black and White Women and the Struggle for Professional Identity**. Boston: Harvard Business School Press, 2003.

Leadership: How to Lead, How to Live

Chapter 8

Starting Our Careers

Being a leader is like being a lady, if you have to go around telling people you are one, you aren't.

- Margaret Thatcher, British prime minister

Whether we are just leaving school or have been working for a few years or both, many of us are about to start the careers that we hope will take us to positions of prominent leadership. We confront many choices. We can choose to work in a large organization or a small one, or even start our own; we can choose to take a line or staff position in a large organization; or we can choose to work in a for-profit or not-for-profit organization, or in a government agency.

In this chapter we'll examine each of these options. Our purpose isn't to point to a particular choice as the right one, because people differ greatly in what they want, in their circumstances, and therefore in what will fit them. But by examining the characteristics of the opportunities facing us, we can improve the choices we make and increase our chance of making choices that turn out right for us.

───────❖───────

Starting our Careers

Small Versus Large Organizations

Small organizations differ from large organizations in many ways. Often people focus on the differences in benefits, pay levels, and employment security. But as managers seeking to advance our careers, the differing challenges and opportunities presented by companies in various stages of growth are very different, and the personality and skills needed and required of the professionals who choose to work in one or the other environment are often different.

So we might ask: What are the pros and cons of working for a large rather than a small company?

People who have worked for smaller firms often report that they found the smaller firm provided opportunities to take on more responsibility, as well as offering more exposure to senior management. The level of exposure in a small company is bigger; the freedom one has to make decisions is also often bigger, but with that comes a lot more responsibility. This is not to say that opportunities and exposure cannot be obtained in a large corporation, but it is often more difficult given the additional layers of administration that exist in larger firms.

On the other side of the coin, smaller organizations normally don't have procedures and processes in place, so one needs to deal with disorder and uncertainty. There is no "hiding" in smaller companies the way there can be in large firms. Big companies also ordinarily have more robust training systems; they better define rewards and expectations; they offer easier changes of job, functionally and geographically, if one seeks them. There are tremendous resources in a large company for an ambitious person who can use his or her imagination to gain access to them.

Another question that is often raised: If a person initially goes to a small company, how hard is it for he or she later to move to a large company?

It is usually much easier to move from a big company to a smaller one than the other way around. Finding a job at a larger company after working at a smaller one means spending a lot of time selling the larger firm on our talents, skills, and accomplishments, because often there is no brand recognition associated with the smaller company. Someone going from General Electric, for example, to a small firm carries with him or her the strong reputation of the big firm, and is likely to be presumed to have the necessary capabilities to perform a job in the smaller company well.

Future Considerations

What about the future? Are our appetites for working for a smaller company, which may be riskier than working for a large company, likely to decline as we move into later stages of our lives?

People are less likely to make important changes in their lives as they get older. Age itself isn't the reason, but rather that we have more commitments—and more other people who are involved in the decision. A young person who is married and the parent of a young child finds his or her penchant for risk declining compared to what it was when he or she was single. Yet, there is not always a straight line from risk-taking to conservatism. That same young person, in another twenty years, when the children are out of school and on their own, may again consider more risky ventures.

Not-for-Profit Versus For-Profit Organizations

Many people seek work in the not-for-profit sector of our economy. It is a large sector of the economy, and includes private organizations such as museums, hospitals, social service organizations, charitable foundations, clubs, as well as very large business enterprises such as the New York Stock Exchange, and large non-governmental regulators such as the National Association of Securities Dealers. Some not-for-profits have a mission that is clearly for the public good; others simply serve a private group but don't seek profits.

For-profit firms exist primarily to earn a financial return for shareholders—profit is that return. Not-for-profits have no such objective; in fact, they explicitly reject it. Instead, many not-for-profit organizations have a mission to contribute in some way to the public good: A museum seeks to preserve and display artwork or historical artifacts for the benefit of the public; a not-for-profit hospital (there are numerous for-profit hospitals) provides health care for the public; the Red Cross provides emergency medical and other assistance to people in times of disaster. They are chartered by state governments to pursue these public purposes. There is a different type of commitment involved in not-for-profit organizations than that expected in for-profit firms.

People often think of not-for-profits in terms of public service missions. They assume that not-for-profits are run by well-intentioned people trying to do good. Although this is the case, it's not the whole story. Many people are disappointed to discover that not-for-profits are managed like for-profit firms. Not-for-profits have a legal and ethical responsibility to their contributors to use their resources honestly, so they adopt businesslike methods. It's an important challenge for leaders

173

in not-for-profit organizations to get others in the organization to see the need for businesslike behavior.

Not-for-profit organizations have managerial positions just as for-profit firms do. They develop plans and budgets, and often have strategic plans; they rely on compensation and personnel systems. In fact, not-for-profit organizations appear very much like for-profit organizations except (and it remains a very big exception), not-for-profits perform a different function in our society.

Recently a for-profit firm that was growing rapidly identified a not-for-profit organization in the same industry as a potential acquisition. The not-for-profit firm, while much larger and older, found itself in financial difficulty; it was spending more money than it could get in fees for its services, and was unable to raise enough money in contributions to offset its deficit. Unless things changed financially, the not-for-profit would have to close or be sold.

When the executives of the for-profit firm discussed acquiring the not-for-profit with their own firm's board of directors and with consultants, the opinion was unanimous that it would be a mistake. The not-for-profit, it was said, would have a very different culture among its managers and employees, one that paid little attention to cost control or customer satisfaction, and virtually none to profitability.

But the executives of the for-profit firm knew something that none of its directors or advisers knew. They had partnered with the not-for-profit for six months on a major project, and had worked with people at all levels and in all parts of the organization. They had realized that while the not-for-profit as a whole operated differently, with a lack of concern for costs, most of the organization was managed just as if it were a for-profit firm—on a budget that managers were expected to adhere to. So, in fact, there was little difference in culture between that part of the not-for-profit of most interest to them, and their own for-profit firm.

So against all advice, the executives of the for-profit firm acquired the not-for-profit. The merger of the two cultures went smoothly because, in reality, the central parts of the two organizations were not that different—and the combined company became a huge success in the marketplace.

Some Similarities And Differences

In general, the not-for-profit and for-profit sectors of American industry are much more similar than people realize. Once the head of a large university was discussing how it was managed. "We are a not-for-profit corporation," he explained. "We don't maximize profit." He paused, then smiled and added, "We maximize the DBIO."

"What," a listener asked, "is the DBIO?"

"It's the difference between income and outgo," the speaker replied.

This was, of course, a small joke. Defined that way, the DBIO would be called a profit in the for-profit world. In the not-for-profit world, it's called a surplus. It's perfectly legal for a not-for-profit firm to earn a surplus, but it isn't legally a profit, and the laws require that different things be done with the surplus (the DBIO) than with a profit.

There are three major differences between a not-for-profit and a for-profit organization, and in the United States two of the three are declining in importance:

Mission: A not-for-profit has a public service purpose of some nature, which, consequently, is what its trustees must pursue with the resources—financial, human, and physical—it has; a for-profit, however, has the objective of earning profits for its shareholders, which remains the responsibility of both the board of directors of the corporation and the corporation's executives. But even this isn't as great a difference as it seems, because many not-for-profits try to generate a surplus and many for-profits have missions to better the world (such as developing and bringing medical devices to people who need them, providing safe and reliable transportation in the form of automobiles) that could serve as missions for a not-for-profit.

The difference is therefore not that a not-for-profit has a public mission and a for-profit doesn't. It's that a not-for-profit is legally required to give first priority to its public mission, and a for-profit to the financial interests of its shareholders. Yet in practice, these distinctions disappear: Not-for-profits must pay attention to their finances even if their missions suffer; and for-profits will often put the interests of their executives, customers, and employees above those of their shareholders

Organizational Culture: The culture of not-for-profits is expected to be different than for-profit firms. The expectation is that there is more concern for the public welfare in a not-for-profit than in a for-profit firm. People working in not-for-profits see themselves as focusing on the public good; those working in for-profits focus on making money. This remains generally the case.

Competition: There is a perception that not-for-profits cannot succeed financially without gifts, so they cannot survive in the highly competitive for-profit world. But this is less obvious than before. Many parts of our economy that traditionally have been the exclusive preserve of not-for-profits now find for-profit firms entering and competing with not-for-profits, including higher education, hospitals, and, on a lesser scale, museums. The result is that not-for-profits are competing head-on with for-profits in the same industries, and must be increasingly competitive to survive.

In the end, a not-for-profit is a different legal form for an organization than a for-profit. In some instances this means that the not-for-profit is more mission-oriented, more publicly concerned, and more fragile economically (meaning that it doesn't earn its way by sales to the public, but must rely to a large or small degree on charitable gifts) than a for-profit firm.

Career Issues

From the point of view of careers, there is less difference than is generally thought between not-for-profits and for-profit firms. Not-for-profits may claim less of one's time and attention than some of the more aggressive for-profit firms, and some of their leaders' responsibilities, such as raising money from donors, take a lot of time and energy and do not exist in the for-profit world.

But there is a hierarchy of management in both not-for-profits and for-profit firms; there are career ladders; there are opportunities to demonstrate leadership, which grow in scope with higher-level positions. These crucial things do not differ between not-for-profits and for-profit firms.

Hence, there is considerable opportunity for a person to exhibit leadership in a not-for-profit, including in salaried positions in the organization.

Line Versus Staff Positions

There's an important distinction between types of positions in a business that had its origins in the military. The distinction is between line and staff positions. A military line position is one commanding troops ("the line") in action; a staff position is one advising commanders on how to accomplish objectives. Both are important. Staff officers collect information (military intelligence), evaluate it, and prepare plans from it. A modern army is a very complex organization, needing many different functional specializations among its personnel and requiring many different kinds of weapons. Keeping it supplied is a tremendous task. Coordinating its movement becomes a very complicated task. The role of staff officers is to plan these things carefully so that the army can advance without being held up by supply shortages or internal conflict (over, for example, the use of a single road by different military units).

Business similarly has line and staff positions. Line positions are those involved in the production and sale of products or services. Staff positions support those managers in line roles. Manufacturing and sales are line functions. Legal, personnel management, logistics, purchasing, and strategic planning are staff functions. A manufacturing manager or a sales manager is a line manager; a personnel manager, purchasing manager, or a manager of a strategic planning department is a staff manager.

In a line role a person is likely to feel somewhat much more accountable than in a staff role because a line manager's work directly affects the company's profitability (its bottom line). A staff role, however, provides a deep understanding of the fundamentals of the company's core business. Staff experience can provide a great deal of credibility with colleagues when a manager switches from a staff role to a line role. So important are both line and staff roles in a large organization that it's difficult to be an effective leader without having experienced both.

As we plan our careers, which do we seek?

Advantages of Line Positions

Line positions often provide invaluable learning of a type not easily obtained in school or even in staff positions. A line manger learns how to respond to customers when they are pressuring him from all sides; how to energize employees who aren't motivated by money or promotions and who don't care who you are or what you learned in school; what it feels like to have an key role in actually making or providing something that satisfies a tangible customer need; and what to do first (that is, how to prioritize one's actions) when, for example, an employee cuts his finger off in a machine.

Experiences like these add to the broad character of a person and fit her for top leadership; top leaders who are looking for successors seek people who have these kinds of experiences, recognizing their importance. Line experience therefore is often necessary to reach a position of highest authority within an organization. Line positions alone can take one to the top of an organization, albeit with unfortunate consequences in some cases that we will identify shortly.

Ordinarily, experience in staff positions alone will not take one to the top of an organization. There are exceptions, but they are few and notable. Usually, it's the line manager who signed up new customers and whose team set sales records who is considered as a candidate for the top job, not the vice president for corporate strategy, or the vice president of human resources or the head of the legal department—all three of whom are high-level staffers.

Yet there is no better place to learn about an organization than from a key staff position. There a person has the responsibility of learning how things are done; of determining the major trends in the marketplace and among competitors; or deciding courses of action. In a sense it is the staff person who often decides what to do; the line manager who carries out the plan.

It is surprising, but possible, to get to a top position in an organization via line management without fully understanding the organization's overall situation. Some dramatic examples of this disconnect occur in the military. For example, during the First World War, many line generals grew accustomed to ordering direct attacks in the face of overwhelming defensive weaponry—and the result was massive casualties. Staff officers began to realize that with the new weapons of war (machine guns and high explosive artillery shells) mass assaults had become suicidal in nature. Sadly, many line officers never fully comprehended this.

In business similar things occur. It's not unusual for sales executives to get to the top positions in companies with skills that are basically motivational (they know how to motivate salespeople to work hard, and to sell imaginatively), but these same executives are not able to comprehend sudden large shifts in customer demand.

Perhaps the most famous example of this in recent business history involves IBM Corporation. For decades IBM had been one of the most successful companies in the world. In the 1980s it was routinely selected as the best-managed company in the world. IBM was an unusual company because it was widely believed to be a technology company, yet its greatest strengths were in marketing and sales. It was the combination of the two that made it extraordinary.

By the 1980s it was the practice at IBM that the CEO came from sales. IBM was a company in the high-technology industry headed by salespeople. Technology people were considered staff; the sales people were line.

At the time IBM was producing very large computers called mainframes and selling them at large profits. Suddenly, there were technological innovations in the industry. First the minicomputer appeared; then the micro—now called the personal computer. IBM thought these new computers were toys. A host of new companies appeared to produce and sell minis and micros. IBM largely ignored them. Its top officers pressed sales managers to meet their targets for mainframes, but sales began to wane. When top salespeople insisted to the top executives of the corporation that it wasn't a failure of effort on the part of the sales staff, but that something else was going on in the marketplace, they were fired.

Staff work at IBM was inadequate to identify the technological shifts going on in the marketplace, and when some glimpse of the truth was gained, top executives quickly dismissed it as not important. IBM continued building manufacturing plants to produce more mainframes, but couldn't sell them. Finally, reality intruded by virtue of huge financial losses to the company; staff work identified the problems and new top executives redirected the company's efforts to new types of products and services, and did so successfully.

It is because of the need for careful analysis of a changing business situation, and careful planning to meet the challenges, that staff functions are so important. Strategic-planning staff analyze and plan for responses to market changes; personnel staff analyze the changing labor market and plan for how to hire good people and how to compensate them; logistics staff determine how to adjust to changing energy prices; legal staff determine how to protect the firm as laws and court decisions change.

In recent years companies have contracted out many more staff planning functions than they had in the past. Large consulting firms have emerged to meet this demand. In effect, consulting firms today perform much of the staff work that used to be performed in companies. Thus, when people look to consulting firms as a place to start their careers, they are in a sense choosing a staff function. So common have external consultants become in large companies that some define a corporate staffer as essentially an internal consultant with less freedom, but typically more authority, than an external consultant.

Other Advantages of Staff Positions

Staff positions can propel a young manager into a position of high impact quickly, providing frequent interaction ("face time") with top management and fast learning about the company as a whole. These are important advantages.

But staff managers don't get to implement their own suggestions; they don't get to see the direct results of their own work; they get little recognition (it's the manufacturing manager who turns out the new products with good quality and reasonable costs; it's the sales manager who hits new sales targets, who gets the recognition and financial rewards); and worst of all, staff managers may find themselves confined in that role and may never be allowed to assume a line position.

In general, the longer a person stays in a staff role, the harder it is to move into a line role (or back into a line role, if she's been there before). This may not be due to an actual deficit in the person's skills, but rather due to the organization's perception of his skills as being limited to those of a staffer.

What Makes a Good Entrepreneur?

In the U.S. many people want to run their own businesses. We generally admire the initiative it takes to become one's own boss. Whether a person's own business is a small shop or the beginnings of a huge company, money can often be raised to start the effort.

There is a large and complex support industry for people starting businesses. At one end are venture capital firms that exist to finance people who want to start businesses with high-growth potential. For people who want to start their own small business without big-time potential, there are also ways to obtain money, usually by borrowing.

Working in a company that we own is not the same thing as working for either a big or small company owned by someone else. Many people think that if a person works for himself, he'll have greater control over his schedule and more time for family and friends. This is, however, unlikely. Working for ourselves is often more demanding than working for others. Sometimes we can't get away from the business at all; when it's in trouble, we have to devote all our time to it.

A special case involves entrepreneurship—starting a business from nothing with the intent of growing it into a large and successful business. Entrepreneurship involves creating something out of nothing. It often attracts people who love to empower others; who want to learn fast and grow a lot in what they do

(For the key qualities of an entrepreneur, see Executive Summary 8-1.)

EXECUTIVE SUMMARY 8-1
KEY QUALITIES OF AN ENTREPRENEUR

The key qualities in an entrepreneur include:

- Ability to focus on a single objective (some people refer to this quality as an almost pathological interest in one thing).

- Commitment to long, very difficult, and all-consuming work (usually a deep passion for the business is necessary for a person to make such a commitment).

- Willingness to do many different tasks (because there is no support staff in a start-up).

- High tolerance for risk (most new businesses fail); less concern for personal financial security.

- Ability to sell self and company (the key to success is getting financial support and customers).

- Ability to quickly seize opportunities and change course if necessary (a plan is useful but probably has to be altered frequently).

- Persistence (there are likely to be many reversals and times when the new company is on the brink of collapse).

- Great degree of tolerance for confusion, chaos, and ambiguity at the workplace (the initial stages of building a business tend to be very disorganized).

Many are attracted to entrepreneurship because there can be enormous payoffs—successful entrepreneurs can become very wealthy and influential. There is a long, difficult path to that success, however. An entrepreneur has to struggle to keep the company growing—getting customers, adding people and other resources, and raising money. She has very little in the way of support in the company.

When a manager in a large firm needs new office space for an expanding department, she calls the firm's real estate office to find space and equip it for her; then her department moves. In contrast, when an entrepreneur needs a larger space for her expanding small company, she calls real estate agents herself, visits various sites she might want, selects one, negotiates the lease with the owner, fights with the phone company to get phones installed within a reasonable time period, goes to the new office to receive shipments of office furniture, and waits for the delivery truck when it's late.

In a large company when a manager needs to fill a position in his department, he writes a job description, sends it to the human resources staff, who advertise the job, interview selected candidates, and send him only a few who have been well screened in advance. The manager then meets two or three candidates, picks one, and informs the human resources department. HR specialists discuss salary and benefits with the prospective employee, and if they reach agreement, the person is hired, receives an orientation, and reports to work to the manager one day.

It isn't like this in a start-up firm. Every new hire is so important—when there are so few employees—that the entrepreneur herself draws up the job description, has it posted online and published in the relevant newspapers and other publications, and tries to get information from a variety of sources about what to pay whoever is chosen for the job. Then she carefully reads all the résumés that are submitted; chooses people to interview; meets them herself, finding some unsuitable from the outset and wishing she'd not wasted her time.

When she finds a desirable candidate, she negotiates pay, usually offering about one-half what the candidate has been making in his last job, and promising that if the company does well, he'll get pay increases and some small amount of ownership in the firm; and she tells him that while he has a specific position, he will be expected to do other things as well, including sales, buying office supplies, fixing broken furniture—all the things that a start-up company has no staff for and no money to hire expensive people from the outside to do.

The role of an entrepreneur is often all-consuming, time-demanding, and emotionally-draining. One of the most successful business builders in America recently told a group of young people (who were considering starting their own businesses) that being an entrepreneur was equivalent in unpleasantness to serving time in prison or getting a horrible disease.

Routes to Entrepreneurship

People who become entrepreneurs take different routes to get there. Some start a new company early in their working lives, and often fail several times before succeeding. For example, Larry Ellison had six failed start-ups in his past before founding Oracle.

Others recognize that they have a lot to learn and choose to learn as much as they can on other people's money. So they work for a big organization while learning the business, then when they feel

Starting our Careers

ready they branch out on their own. Rather than start a new venture early, they wait ten years or so after finishing school. By then, they have a good sense of the industry in which they've been working; have cultivated relationships with other people that enable them to raise funds and obtain initial customers; and have saved up some capital to invest in their own companies. They have gained street smarts in business and feel better able to start a successful business.

These are the two major types of entrepreneurs:

The *"born" entrepreneur* who doesn't want to work for anyone else ever, and who starts company after company (sometimes succeeding, sometimes failing); this type is not likely ever to work for a large organization no matter what she might learn.

The *"made" entrepreneur* who works for a big company and then sees an opportunity, leaves the big company to start a company of his own, and attempts to use his skills, network of contacts, and other advantages from his time at the big company to advance his start-up.

For people in the second category, a key question is: When is the best time to take the big risk of starting our own company? There is a great advantage to waiting for a number of years while we gain experience and contacts at a big firm; but, if we also acquire a family, a house and mortgage payment, some hobbies we enjoy, then the risks associated with becoming an entrepreneur may become too high to accept. Said a young man considering starting a company of his own, "I'd rather risk myself and my fiancée now than risk my wife and three children later."

When a person is young, with relatively few financial and relational responsibilities, when any mistakes she makes now are less likely to have an impact than when she is older, then the time

187

might seem ideal for starting a firm. But, on the other hand, if she waits, then her knowledge and experience may make the success of her company much more likely.

CHAPTER REFERENCES:

Gerstner, Louis. **Who Says Elephants Can't Dance?** New York: HarperBusiness, 2002.

ADDITIONAL READINGS:

Harvard Business Review on Leadership. Boston: Harvard Business School Press, 1998.

Watkins, Michael. **The First Ninety Days: Critical Success Strategies for New Leaders at all Levels.** Boston: Harvard Business School Press, 2003.

Leadership: How to Lead, How to Live

Chapter 9

Advancing Along the Path to Leadership

The world will belong to passionate, driven leaders—people who not only have enormous amounts of energy but who can energize those whom they lead.

- Jack Welch, former General Electric CEO

Leadership: How to Lead, How to Live

The previous chapter discussed the broad considerations in planning a career, including whether to seek a position in a small versus a large organization, in a for-profit versus a not-for-profit organization, a place in the line or the staff of an organization, or even being an entrepreneur. In this chapter we discuss finding the right job in which to start.

When we interview for a job, it's important to realize that the organization is looking for a new employee, just as we're looking for a job, so while the organization is deciding whether or not to choose us, we are also deciding whether or not to choose it.

What to Look For in an Organization

Some of us will want to start our careers in small companies; some in large firms; others will want to work in nonprofit organizations. All these are established organizations with established ways of doing things and common attitudes among the people working for them (what we term the "culture" of a firm). How do we choose among them? What is it that we are looking for in an organization?

An important thing to look for is growth in the company and growth in the industry. Clearly a growing company has more opportunities for advancement. Conversely a company that is declining, or is likely to begin declining because its industry is weakening, will likely be laying people off, so a person will be trying to gain promotions in a very difficult environment—not impossible, but difficult. A declining company also is likely to be reducing budgets, so people have less and less to work with in terms of resources.

But if one is passionate about entering an industry in decline, one shouldn't completely rule it out. More important than where the industry is going may be the focus of the company. Many companies seek to reinvent themselves. If one can find a company with a comfortable culture that wants to overcome its challenges (whether that be by growing in a shrinking market or reinventing itself completely), there can be real opportunity for a motivated manger.

It may be more difficult to find a solid company in a declining industry, and taking on a position in such a company can involve more risk. Certainly an industry in a steep decline is much more dangerous than one in a slower decline. Finally, there is something to going somewhere or doing something that nobody else wants to do. This strategy can quickly make a person a pretty big fish in a small pond.

Instead of entering a growth industry, we can seek to find a high-growth company in a strong industry. Thus, if we can find a great role with potential for high impact in a high-growth company, we have tremendous room for impact and can learn a lot at the same time. Many wildly successful people have entered low-growth industries because they saw an opportunity to change the way the economic game was played in those industries and, consequently, had tremendous impact. That being said, if we should face a choice between entering a company that is trying to capture a share of a growing pie, versus joining a company which has to steal a share of a shrinking pie from its competitors, the former is definitely a more attractive situation.

Industry Considerations

For many of us, however, the industry in which we work has little significance. A person who took a job in media, thinking that he'd love it, found that he did like his job but not because of the industry. The company could have been selling anything, for all he cared. What he enjoyed were the people with whom he worked, the tasks he was given to do, and the high level of responsibility he had. Many employment counselors often advise people that the most important thing in a job is *what* a person will be doing, and not the industry, product, or growth rate of the firm.

For example, every holiday season the managers and executives of L. L. Bean Company in Freeport, Maine, arrive at work at 5:30 a.m. in order to work for several hours before the start of the regular workday to wrap presents customers have ordered. This is fun for them, and although it represents extra work and is time-consuming, it's a reason some people give for working at the company.

Choosing where to start a career is a very important decision for each of us. It's important to study different opportunities, but sometimes we can over-rationalize our decisions. If we look around, we're likely to know when we've found the right fit. Of course, we'll come up with a host of reasons why it's the rational choice for us. We probably would not be attracted to a particular course of action if it did not fit some rational criteria in the first place.

What's important is that we think about what we want to get out of a position before accepting it, and are willing to leave if it is not leading in the direction we wish to go.

Choosing a Job

It's very important in choosing a job in the early stages of our careers to explore each opportunity well beyond its financial aspects. We're looking for a start in a process that will meet our general career goals, and we're expecting to be making additional decisions about steps on a career path as we go. We intend to be flexible in our decision-making because we're always working toward our career goals, even if our path may turn out to be a bit indirect. Hence, it's important to know more about the organization we'll join than just what job it offers us.

For many of us comfort in our jobs involves a number of moral and social considerations, not just the salary and tasks of a job. We need to discover where an organization stands on issues that matter to us. This can be difficult because companies often don't readily disclose such matters.

For large organizations we can often look into such matters in their publications, on their Web sites, or in media accounts about the organization. For smaller companies it's more difficult, and we may simply have to inquire about them in the interview process. It is a distinct advantage that in a smaller organization we are likely to be interviewed by one of the top executives, and can ask directly. In a large organization, we'll probably be interviewed by a personnel officer responsible for interviewing, who may be uncomfortable with such questions; hence the importance of doing background research about the organization.

Choosing a Boss

When we interview for a job in a small organization, we may actually talk to the boss. However, when we interview in a large organization, we're likely to first be interviewed by a personnel or HR staffer, but if we pass that screening, we may well have an interview with the person who will be our boss.

What do we want when we choose a boss? At the start of our careers we want someone who will help us learn and grow in the job. We are apprentice leaders, not merely people looking for a paycheck, and so the personal development we obtain in a job is crucial to us. Developmental opportunity should be more important to us than pay. But most of us will want a person who will be pleasant to work with, because if that's not the case, then we may get sidetracked from learning and growing in the job.

Sometimes, when introducing students to job opportunities, schools will bring executives to campus to meet with large groups of students. Sometimes the visitors are likable; but sometimes not. Generally, if a visitor isn't likable people will say, "I couldn't work for him." But some people will take a different tack. They'll say, "I don't really like him, but I could learn so much working for him that I want to do it if I can get the job."

Advancing Along the Path to Leadership

We should beware first impressions. Some people who are unimpressive on first meeting can turn out to be effective leaders because of other positive traits; some people who are charismatic can be poor leaders because of other flaws. It's useful to have a second meeting, if possible, with a potential boss. It may be difficult to discipline ourselves to do this, however. After all, we've met the boss and liked her; and the organization is offering us the job. We'll be tempted to just take it. But we're likely to have a few questions left, so we could ask to just briefly see the person again. If the boss has no time for us, that tells us something. She may have said in our first interview that she'll work closely with us, and we thought, "That's great, because then I can learn so much." But if she hasn't even got time for a brief second meeting, it's not likely she's going to have much time for us when we are on the job.

If we do get a second visit, then we get to see if she greets us with the same personality as before. On the first visit, she may have been at pains to be charming. This time, she might be impatient, abrupt, or show other qualities that are less attractive and might suggest that working with her will be less enjoyable than we thought. Alternatively, she might be even more accessible and charming, really welcoming us to her team.

Finally, there's always the chance that asked the same question a second time, the boss will give a different answer; and do so several times. This would be a major red flag, indicating that he is simply making up answers that he thinks we want to hear, or that he gets confused about what he has said before.

What are we looking for when we interview a potential boss? We should look for her to be excited about her role and what we might contribute to her team; for in-depth knowledge about the activities she oversees and what they are for; for clear recognition of her strengths and weaknesses; for an ability to see the bigger picture regarding the role of her department in the organization; for a comfortable and inclusive style of managing relationships with others; and for willingness and skill in helping us learn.

Getting Good Advice

When one of us unfortunately has a boss with whom we don't get along, we shouldn't fight with the person, nor is it a good strategy to try harder to perform well in hope of changing his view of us. Instead, we should try to get out of his department. A constructive approach is to very politely thank him for all that we've learned from him (if anything) and say "I want to get a transfer to continue to learn and grow." He's likely to let us go, and we've created no animosity by the way we approached moving on in our careers.

As we start out on our path to top leadership positions, it's important to get good advice. We are likely to be too busy to figure some important things out by ourselves. When we are getting started in our careers, we seem to be always rushing from one thing to another—whether it is making important decisions such as what job to take or where to live or as trivial as juggling all our different daily obligations (exercising, volunteering, job interviews, receptions, and parties.)

For advice we should turn to people we trust, including younger people who seem to be making good progress in their careers, and more experienced people we might know through our families, houses of worship, or similar settings. The special case of mentors in organizations is discussed below.

Advancing Along the Path to Leadership

What kind of advice should we seek? In general, there are two kinds of advice: specific, up-to-the-minute advice about what to do now, and more general, longer-perspective advice about how to craft our path ahead. For specific advice, we should look to people close to our current job setting; for longer-term advice, we should look to experienced people who have reflected about what they've done themselves in climbing an organizational ladder or in building a company from the ground up. With experienced and introspective people as advisors we are listening to people who have thought deeply about the issues and whose words reflect a clear understanding of the meaning of their experiences.

The views of less experienced people, even if those people are already successful, are likely to be "works in progress" because they simply have not experienced enough and thought deeply enough about the experiences to have it all down. People still much engaged in building their own careers are likely not to have a very well thought out understanding of themselves. Similarly they may be somewhat uncertain regarding what is important in life; for example, a blind commitment to work at the expense of having any meaningful relationships may suggest immaturity. On the other hand, a blind commitment to relationships at the expense of work may suggest naiveté. What we want in an advisor for the long term is someone who can help keep us grounded and focused.

Mentors and Formal Mentoring Programs

Mentoring makes advice more formal; it establishes an ongoing relationship between two people who recognize a responsibility to each other. The responsibility of the mentor is to advise; the responsibility of the person being advised (the "mentee") is to take advice seriously and do his or her best to use it successfully. Mentoring was unusual and the term was little recognized until two decades ago; now the term is familiar to many people and large organizations often have adopted formal mentor programs.

A mentor is a person who knows from experience much about an organization and how a person new to it should conduct him- or herself for success. The mentor agrees to help the mentee in the organization; the two agree to meet periodically and to stay in touch via emails or phone calls more frequently. The mentor will answer the mentee's questions, and advise him or her when it is appropriate. The mentor should spend enough time with the mentee to get to know his or her strengths and weaknesses, and advise on how to capitalize on strengths and correct weaknesses. The mentor should also suggest germane development efforts to the mentee: training programs, short-term assignments, shifts of job, and so on. There are few better ways than mentoring for newcomers to learn from the mistakes of the past, in the hopes of avoiding them in the future.

Excellent organizations in most fields of endeavor have embraced systems of mentoring. In the U.S., one of a military commander's primary responsibilities is to provide leadership development to his or her junior officers and groom them to be future commanders. The performance and development of one's subordinates is often seen as a direct reflection on the effectiveness of the leader/supervisor and his or her coaching and mentoring. In some private sector for-profit organizations, progress in developing the careers of young managers through mentoring of one form or another has become a specific factor in the annual evaluation of senior executives used to determine bonuses. Not surprisingly, when a portion of compensation is attached to performance as a mentor, the responsibility gets more attention from senior managers.

Advancing Along the Path to Leadership

Formal mentoring programs work well if there is proper focus and attention from an organization's leaders and if people are held accountable. Ineffective formal mentoring usually results from a lack of focus from the top, a "check-the-box" (rather than "do-the-task-well") mentality, and a lack of training and accountability for top executives.

Many organizations provide a formal mentoring program, assigning a mentor to a new manager, or expecting the new person to look for and recruit a mentor herself. But there is a division of opinion about formal mentoring programs. Many top executives think that newcomers are better off developing informal relationships with senior managers, rather than being assigned a mentor by the company. They think the formal system is too formal; that it often connects people who don't have good personal "chemistry"; and that because it is formal, it gets treated like a chore rather than a serious endeavor. If a person who is assigned as a mentor does not view a mentee as a valuable part of the community (e.g., as a "go-getter" or "self-starter"), then the mentor will be far less likely to devote time to the person.

For example, one summer a young person worked at an organization that values mentoring. She had two mentors assigned to her—one only slightly more senior than she was and one who was significantly more senior. Although both people were diligent about fulfilling their duties and genuinely cared about how she was faring in the company, she was not able to establish a strong personal connection with either one. Instead, she found that the more informal relationships she built over the months provided much more useful feedback, advice, and perspective on the firm. In addition, she felt more comfortable expressing her thoughts about the job and the culture to her unofficial mentors.

Critics of formal mentoring programs point out that the greatest benefit of an informal mentoring program is precisely that—it is not required, so it involves a senior person willingly taking someone under her wing to help his development and help him move forward both within the organization and as a person.

Informal mentoring in which each new manager finds his or her own mentor may be fine if the new manager is part of the dominant group in the organization, but if one is a minority, it can be more difficult "to be taken under the wing." In this case, to ensure equal opportunity, a formal mentoring program can be useful. A well-designed mentoring program, therefore, can improve the diversity and inclusiveness of an organization, as well as providing an excellent avenue for senior people to pass on practical advice to junior staff.

Formal mentoring programs can be valuable in helping people develop for two reasons:

- Mentoring allows newcomers to integrate into the organization in a formal way thorough a structured program and then, if desired/adequate, through informal connections and mentoring. Over time, the nature of mentoring is likely to change. A formal program either turns into a personal and informal enduring relationship between mentor and mentee, or it declines into uselessness as the mentee develops new informal mentors or is, unfortunately, left out.

- There is benefit for the more senior staff who become mentors in that they have to learn how to guide someone effectively through her or his career within the organization. Skills of this nature in working with other people become increasingly relevant as a person's career advances toward top positions, and being a mentor helps establish such skills.

But, no matter how an organization attempts to promote a mentoring program or enforce the obligation of its senior managers to participate in it, any mentoring program must be primarily mentee-driven. If the mentee doesn't take the lead in committing to the program, then formal meetings may occur as required, but the impact on the mentee's development will be insignificant.

Ideally, a mentor is a senior person with whom a junior person can be completely candid and from whom he or she can seek advice when facing difficult choices or problems. A mentor should always tell the truth and recognize when a mentee is not being honest with him- or herself. All of this requires solid trust-based relationships and goes beyond purely formal corporate processes.

A person new to an organization is especially fortunate if there is in place not only a formal mentoring program but a program of mentor education, which educates both mentors and mentees about what makes a good mentor. Then senior staffers who serve as mentors know how to do a good job, and perhaps more importantly, junior people know what to expect from a mentor. A problem with formal mentoring programs left to run alone, without such an education effort, is that when a junior person gets a bad mentor, he or she may not even realize what is missing.

Another key issue to consider in mentoring is the extent of responsibility of the mentor. The key responsibility of the mentor is giving advice, because this is common to all mentoring. But sometimes the person being mentored has a much broader notion of the responsibility of the mentor, and sometimes mentors accept the broader responsibility.

In essence, the broader responsibility of the mentor may not just be for advice, but for advancing the mentee's career within the organization. In effect, the mentor becomes a sponsor for the mentee within the organization. As a sponsor, the mentor does several things that go far beyond giving advice—including recommending the mentee for assignments or promotions, steering the mentee through personal or political conflicts within the organization, and championing the mentee for recognition within the organization. In effect, the mentor becomes the champion of the mentee's career.

Often the people who recruit us to an organization can be excellent mentors; and sometimes they'll be sponsors for us. If you're in a small company, make a special effort to have some mentors from outside the company since the range of advice from a mentor within the company may be somewhat limited.

Such an extension of the mentor's role has both good and bad aspects. On the positive side, a mentor who is well positioned and either well respected or powerful in the organization can do a great deal to advance a mentee's career. He is likely to know when choice career assignments are to be filled, or when advantageous promotions are coming up. He can put in a word for his mentee, and sometimes help get him or her the job directly.

If the mentee is getting too close to someone else in the organization whose star is fading, the mentor can put in an explanatory word to higher-ups, as well as advising the mentee to put space between himself and the other person. In effect, the mentor can not only advise the mentee where there are political dangers or opportunities in the organization, but he or she can also take actions on behalf of the mentee. This can be extremely helpful, to the extent that mentees sometimes expect mentors to do such things on their behalf automatically.

But having a mentor who goes these extra miles can also be risky. Before long everyone in the organization knows about how close the relationship is between the mentor and mentee. If the mentor should run into some difficulty in her career, the mentee is likely to encounter difficulty too. The mentee is the mentor's person in a way that limits the mentee's freedom of action in the organization.

Furthermore, other people in the organization who might also be qualified to serve in a mentoring role to the person will probably never offer, because the mentee is already known to be very close to the original mentor. In a relationship as close as this, the mentee becomes the protégé of the mentor, which is a different, more complex, and more intimate relationship than normally exists between mentor and mentee.

There Is No Single Path to the Top

The route to the top executive office of large U.S. companies has been broadening rapidly. For Fortune 100 companies, in 1980 all CEOs were men; by 2001, 11 percent were women. In 1980 20 percent of CEOs were from Ivy League schools; by 2001, only 10 percent were; today 48 percent of CEOs of the largest companies are graduates of public colleges.

Top executives are spending fewer years at the companies they lead (twenty years in 1980 and fifteen years in 2001) and only about half of them have worked their entire careers at the company of which they are CEO. (Peter Cappelli and Monika Hamon, "The New Road to the Top," Harvard *Business*

Review, Special Issue, Managing Yourself, January, 2005, pp. 25-32).

Not everything goes well on our way up the corporate ladder. We must be resilient, shaking off our setbacks. Correct whatever we've done wrong quickly, and move on. Many people fail to advance in their careers because they insist on defending bad decisions they've made—fearful to admit that an error has been made. This is the bigger error, not to admit the initial mistake and move on.

Politics in an Organization

Every organization has internal politics, involving a contest among individuals for top spots, and/or a struggle over the direction of the organization. Organizational politics is both personal and policy-oriented—about people (who gets the top positions in the organization or in a unit), and about which way certain things are done (for example, a choice about whether or not to make an acquisition). In some organizations there are intense political struggles; in others, the struggles are muted. Ordinarily top executives try to minimize political wrangling in their organizations because it can take up lots of staff time and energy. Nonetheless, the nature of organizations is that there is some political activity everywhere.

A new manager can get quickly involved in the internal politics of the enterprise, supporting someone else's candidacy for a key job, or supporting a particular direction for the firm, or he or she can try to stay out of these internal battles. If the new manager elects involvement and is on the winning side, it may advance her career; however, if he's on the losing side, it may sidetrack him. Because being on the wrong side of a political controversy can sidetrack a career, it's often best to try to avoid getting drawn into internal politics.

Advancing Along the Path to Leadership

The best way to stay out of organizational politics is to always try to do whatever seems right for the company as a whole. A person can openly profess no interest in the internal politics; if solicited to support one side in an internal political battle, he can say he knows little about it, and then never get around to learning more.

But a person's career can sometimes be damaged by staying above the fray. People who are deeply involved politically will not recognize someone who has been aloof as part of their group, and may divide the best assignments and promotions among themselves, leaving others out. This is an unfortunate aspect of some organizational cultures: top performance alone is often not enough to ensure advancement and being on the "winning side" politically is more important. Simply relying on performance for advancement in an organization will certainly be viewed as naïve by some.

It becomes harder to stay out of political contests as one rises in the hierarchy of an organization. There are many reasons for this—not the least of which is that a high-ranking manager is likely to have influence on the thinking of others, and so is prized by one side or the other of the political contest. The skills of knowing whom to support, how, and when to shift one's support if necessary are best learned by experience and become more important (in fact, become virtually survival skills) as the level of one's position rises.

To avoid getting entangled in company politics:

- Develop an appreciation for the personal angle without personalizing issues.
- Don't view each decision that affects your department adversely as an attempt to undermine your power base. Instead, look for business purpose in the action.

- Don't demonize.

- Don't view people who seem to be trying to outmaneuver you as evil. They're just trying to outmaneuver you as you try to outmaneuver them. But if you encounter a really bad person, be more careful than usual.

(Loren Gray, "Fighting the Enemy Within," *Harvard Management Update*, 7, 2 (February 2002, p. 6.)

Work-Arounds Versus Taking On the Big Issues

We've noted that minorities can confront special barriers in advancing their careers. It is clear that without a formal mentor program, some minorities may fail to get mentors and be disadvantaged in the competition for career advancement. While the evidence is very strong that prejudices of many sorts against minorities have been declining in the United States, they still exist.

There is an important controversy about how a member of a minority group (whether racial, gender, age, religious, or sexual orientation) should react when he or she encounters discrimination.

Work-Arounds

Many successful minorities urge that the proper way to respond to discrimination is to work around it. They offer numerous observations in support of this position:

1. Often it is difficult to be certain that discrimination is actually occurring. For example, there might be two very well qualified candidates for CEO of a firm. One is a minority; one is not. The minority is not chosen. It could be discrimination, but it might not be. How

does one know? If it is indeed discrimination, and the minority candidate believes evidence exists, then there are government agencies to which one can appeal, and that should be done. But often it just isn't clear what happened or whether discrimination occurred. So to assume that the choice was a result of discrimination and complain openly about it runs the risk of alienating many people, some or all of whom may actually be innocent.

2. If discrimination does occur, then it is really the problem of the bigots. It's they who have twisted characters. To focus on the damage done to us by them is to let ourselves get caught in the same psychological jungle they inhabit. It's better for our own mental health to ignore other people's narrow-minded perceptions.

3. It's better, therefore to work hard, try one's best, and move ahead as best we can.

4. Fighting discrimination is essential and is best done in a positive way—by helping develop minority candidates for jobs at all levels of an organization, by offering them opportunities whenever possible, and by working with support groups including providing assistance for complainants when discrimination is blatant.

5. Working around discrimination successfully, and advancing one's career, is one way to answer the bigots and work for general change and improvement. To be successful is to start to disprove prejudice, and to be a role model for others as well until the prejudice breaks down. This approach has positive short-term

personal benefits, as well as longer-term benefits to the larger community.

6. It's not possible to make instantaneous revolutionary changes to ingrained ways of thinking, so the only method that has real potential to effect substantial change is working around prejudice.

Taking On the Big Issues

Critics of working around have very strong arguments as well. They point out that:

1. Unless discrimination is openly challenged it can flourish in the background, damaging the careers of minorities, but never being exposed and extinguished.

2. An open challenge forces other people to take sides, and thereby prevents the sort of silent acquiescence (and hypocrisy) in which discrimination can thrive.

3. An open challenge to injustice from minorities in leadership positions gives hope to people farther down the career ladder that things will get better.

4. A society will never advance unless people openly and dramatically call attention to great evils such as discrimination.

People who are successful and consider themselves leaders are not really behaving as leaders if they try to work around discrimination rather than take it on openly. Leadership isn't about quietly accepting evil, but openly resisting it.

FREQUENTLY ASKED QUESTIONS

Question: *Should I expect to find a mentor?*

Answer: Yes. Only a person who has great difficulty getting along with others should not seek a mentor. In some organizations a mentor will be assigned to a new manager. The advantage of this is that we get a mentor without any effort of our own. But the disadvantage is that the person we get might not be a good mentor, and we also lose the opportunity to choose a mentor ourselves. Choosing one takes longer, and forces us to learn about the people in the organization who might be good mentors. We'd have to go to the person we choose and ask whether he or she would agree to be a mentor for us but we'd have one we'd handpicked.

Question: *If the organization appoints a mentor for me, can I also choose another on my own?*

Answer: In terms of the program, probably yes. But choosing a second formal mentor on one's own could be a mistake. It's likely to embarrass the person appointed to be the mentor; he may think he's been rejected as inadequate, and may think the rest of the organization thinks so too. We could say that we want two mentors, but because the formal program provides only one, the message would seem to be that one is enough. So if we get a mentor we don't like, the best response is to try to get that person to agree to let us find another on our own. The public explanation for such a switch could be that the person assigned to be our mentor is too busy, or is in the wrong part of the organization.

But it may be possible to find an informal mentor to supplement the formal mentor, which may work well. That way a person can have two different sources of opinion—someone assigned to the mentee, who probably would not otherwise have been available, and someone chosen by the mentee.

Question: *How should I find a mentor?*

Answer: Many great leaders like being mentors. For example, if the organization hasn't assigned you a mentor, you can make an appointment with a potential mentor and ask, "Will you talk to me?" If you have a good talk, ask for another. You've got a *de facto* mentor already. After a session or two, ask for a formal mentor relationship.

Question: *Where should I look for a mentor?*

Answer: Look outside your own department, about three levels above you in the organization. That way you can hope to get both objectivity and experience to enrich the advice you get. Look for a person who works well with others, and who is willing to commit the time and effort that being a good mentor requires.

Question: *What are the characteristics of a good mentor, and of a bad one?*

Answer: Bad mentors typically broadcast their advice as universal truths for all to understand and use in their lives. Probably, there are only a few concepts that should and can be presented as universal truths. Instead, good mentoring advice is specific to people and situations and is usually difficult to directly translate from one person's complex life into another person's complex life.

Question: *Can a mentor protect me from mistakes?*

Answer: From some, yes. Particularly with respect to career choices. But the ordinary mistakes of life we are all going to make; what distinguishes us is how much we learn from them, and there a mentor can help.

ADDITIONAL READINGS:

Ciampa, Dan, and Michael D. Watkins. **Right From the Start: Taking Charge in a New Leadership Role.** Boston: Harvard Business School Press, 2003.

Caesar, Vance. **Uncommon Career Success.** Seal Beach, California: PCH Publishing, 2003.

Harvard Business Review on What Makes a Leader. Boston: Harvard Business School Press, 2001.

Maccoby, Michael. **The Productive Narcissist.** New York: Broadway, 2003.

Leadership: How to Lead, How to Live

Chapter 10

Career Hurdles We Create

I'm not afraid of storms, for I'm learning to sail my ship.

- Louisa May Alcott, American author

It is hard enough to pursue a career up the ladder of success toward a position of substantial leadership that we don't need to create additional hurdles for ourselves. But many of us do just that.

The list of career pitfalls we dig is very long.

For example, many of us cannot avoid letting justifiable pride in our accomplishments turn into arrogance. Other people want us to have pride in ourselves but they don't want us to appear arrogant. Often the dividing line between the two attitudes—self-esteem and arrogance—is thin, but the difference is significant.

Connected to arrogance is a know-it-all attitude. Because none of us can begin to know all there is to be known, it has to be a pretense, and is inevitably perceived as such. It's possible to bring a lot of knowledge to bear on business problem solving without pretending to be a know-it-all.

People like to talk about other people; to recount stories about them and to make judgments about them. But though others entice us to join in gossip, they don't admire it when we do, and word often gets back to the people about whom we've been talking. Such events create resentments.

How Reputation Matters

There are lots of things for which we can get bad reputations. We can take the credit for other people's work as our own. Or we can appear greedy, for money or for recognition or advancement. Our peers may think we are too ambitious too early in our careers. We may get a bad reputation as a user of other people, getting them to do things which redound to our credit, not theirs. We may get a reputation for being unkind to others.

It might seem that these are merely personal characteristics, and what really matters is performance on the job. It is true that performance matters, but not to the exclusion of one's personal reputation. At the same time, it can be highly damaging from the perspective of our career prospects to be perceived as performing poorly on the job.

It's unfortunate as well to be thought ungrateful to those who are helping us, whether bosses, mentors, peers, or people who report to us at work.

People notice ethical slips, although they may not talk much about them. We must avoid displaying questionable ethical standards whether in the workplace or outside of it. Most people will not make a differentiation between work and outside of work in the arena of ethics. They will think that a person who isn't moral in one place won't be moral in the other.

Finally, loyalty means a lot in all organizations. Sometimes people focus on loyalty to the organization; sometimes their loyalty is tied to the organization's mission; sometimes to the leaders of the organization; sometimes to peers. Whatever the standard of loyalty is, others treat it as a moral standard of great significance, and it is very important not to transgress in this area.

However, loyalty to a company used to play a much more significant role in careers than it generally does today. People used to remain with the same company most of their working lives, and they and the company both expected that the firm would care for the employee via health insurance and pension when she or he retired. In return, employees were unwilling to leave the firm, even when a better job offer was made to them by another company. And their co-workers expected them to stay with the firm, so that if they left, then they were viewed as traitors. But this set of attitudes has changed. Instead, companies are quick to let people go when there is an opportunity to save money by doing so; and people are quick to leave a firm for a better job elsewhere.

Asked how much loyalty an employee should expect from a company, Jack Welch, former CEO of General Electric, responded, "None." And how much loyalty does a company expect from an employee—not much. Still, it's a bit of a double standard in that an employee who leaves a firm is likely to be viewed as disloyal and not eligible to be rehired. There are exceptions in some industries, including construction, motion pictures, and long-shoring where people often move among employers following available work.

Loyalty to a company in other industries has a place when we

- Have a platform in the company from which to accomplish things that are important to our career development;
- Are treated well by the company; and,
- Have a voice in the firm (that is, are listened to).

So loyalty is an important but uncertain matter. Attitudes toward loyalty—including the degree to which it is expected of an employee—vary greatly among firms. It's important for us to determine what the expectation as to loyalty is at the place we work, and conform to it if possible.

Each item on this long list can imperil our career success. Yet each is something that we can control: We can avoid arrogance, pretense about knowing it all, gossiping, and so on. So to allow ourselves to become identified in other people's minds with any item on this list is merely to erect barriers to our own success. These things are pitfalls we have dug for ourselves, and we begin to spend time and energy trying to avoid falling into them—time and energy we could better spend in an affirmative way advancing our careers.

The Reputation We Want at the Office

We want to avoid the items on the long list of career pitfalls. What is it that we don't want to avoid? What is the reputation we want as we advance in our careers?

At the earliest stage of our career in an organization, when we are newly arrived in the workplace, when we don't know others well, when we are just learning the specifics of the activities of the department, we want to be friendly, accessible, helpful, and grateful.

We want others to think we are fun to be around; that they can interact with us easily; that we try to be helpful to others; and that if they help us, we'll be grateful.

This is not the time to try to impress others with what we know and how effective we are. The reason is that we have so much to learn that we are certain to need direction; if we try to show how smart or effective we are while needing help with almost everything, we are going to look foolish and arrogant.

Because we are interested in progressing up the career ladder, it is wise not to become part of "the gang." While being accessible and friendly, we should steer clear of those who have reached a plateau in their careers and may have developed a less-than-positive attitude.

EXECUTIVE SUMMARY 10-1

CAREER PITFALLS WE DIG FOR OURSELVES

- Appearing arrogant
- Pretending to know it all
- Gossiping about peers
- Getting a bad reputation
  - -for taking others' work as our own
  - -for being greedy
  - -for being too ambitious too early
  - -for using others for our own purposes
  - -for being mean to others
- Performing poorly on the job
- Being ungrateful
- Losing touch
- Displaying questionable ethics
  - -at work
  - -outside work
- Being disloyal
  - -to the organization
  - -to our boss

We should avoid becoming part of "the gang," for if we do, two things will happen.

First, our superiors will notice and wonder if we really are suitable for promotion. They'll wonder: Can she be placed in charge of a group of people with whom she's so close; she looks like one of them—can she discipline and direct them? Will they accept her as a leader? Second, they may conclude that the answer is no to all these questions if we seem to fit in too closely with the group.

Showing What We Can Accomplish

As we learn about the job, then we should begin to show what we can accomplish. This is when our knowledge becomes relevant—as applied in situations as it is needed, not displayed for itself as a sort of medal. We want to stand out to our superiors as people who are hard working, committed, serious, and effective.

When our superiors begin to consider us for promotion, they'll think about our personal qualities. It's good then to show that we are grateful to those who have helped us in the job; that we don't gossip about others; that people are not questioning our morals or ethics, on or off the job.

Sometimes people insist that their private lives are their own—that what they do outside work should be nobody's business, and in one aspect this is right. It should not matter in assessing a person's current job performance what happens outside work. But work performance is only part of our concern, because we're not just trying to keep our current job, we're trying to advance up a ladder of promotion. Those who seek positions of significant leadership know this is part of the assessment process.

Certainly our superiors in an organization are going to take a look at our lives outside the office for two reasons:

- To try to determine what personality traits we have that are likely to be helpful or unhelpful to us in a higher-level position.

- To be sure that if we are promoted and become identified with the organization in the outside community, that our behavior is not going to embarrass the organization.

To a degree, as we make progress in our careers, rising in our organizations, our private lives become less our own. This is a matter of degree and doesn't mean that our superiors have a right to look into intimate aspects of our personal lives. In fact, in recent decades organizations have become far less intrusive into people's personal lives and far more tolerant of a range of private behavior than before, but there are still limits.

Being Nice, Tough and Smart

As we rise higher in our organizations, into positions that require leadership, then how do we want to be perceived? Probably we'd like to be thought of as nice, tough, and smart.

- **Nice** means that we treat people with courtesy and respect; that when we have to discipline a person, we do it in private and politely, rather than yelling at the person across the floor of the office, factory, or trading room.

- **Tough** means that we have high standards for performance and for honesty; that we hold ourselves and others to those high standards; that if there is a crisis, we remain calm and work to solve the problem; that when things are going badly, we keep good spirits and persevere. Tough does not mean nasty or angry or mean. It is perfectly consistent with being nice.

- **Smart** means that we know how to get things done on time and efficiently; that we learn quickly; that we can show others what to do; that we understand what is really going on; that we are imaginative in resolving problems; that when others tell us about situations, we catch on quickly and correctly understand what we're being told.

In our society there need be no difference between men and women in the desirability of this reputation. A man doesn't have to seem tougher than a woman, nor a woman less tough than a man. Furthermore, a woman doesn't have to conceal her intelligence; nor a man his courtesy. These qualities—nice, tough, smart—are business-related qualities, appropriate to people in leadership positions, or aspiring to leadership positions, whatever their gender.

The higher we rise in an organization, the more out of touch we can get with what is happening at the ground-floor level. To prevent this from happening some top executives make a special effort to keep aware. For example, the head of a large hotel chain would work once a year as a bell captain at a hotel, to interact with customers where they first encountered his staff.

The head of a large electronics retail chain spent a thirteen-hour day at a major store during the Christmas season to learn how it felt to be a salesperson and to get firsthand knowledge of the customer experience. He came away noting that his company left many customer needs unsatisfied, and that even so, it was an exhausting job for his company's employees to do retail sales well.

Leadership: How to Lead, How to Live

Leaders need to develop not only a mastery of their immediate functions, but also an awareness of the broader company around them. The situations in a person's own department and company are sometimes called the "retail" environment of the leader; the situation in the broader industry and community is sometimes called the "wholesale" environment of the leader.

Too often managers become expert in their own units, but have no broader perspective. When it comes time to promote them to top leadership positions, they aren't ready and have to be passed over. Ultimately what matters is the situation of the whole organization, not just its various parts.

People working in government learn this rather quickly because of the way citizens and the press reacts to government actions, good and bad. Unfortunately it's possible to do a good job in our part of a company or not-for-profit for years without ever learning much about the broader organization in which we operate. Companies can help their employees escape this trap by a variety of means (see Douglas A. Ready, "How to Grow Great Leaders," *Harvard Business Review*, December, 2004, pp. 93-100.), but the real responsibility lies with each of us as individuals.

An Example of Career Killers in a Specific Company

We have been discussing impediments that we unnecessarily create to career advancement. Our list has been general, but of course in any particular organization there are career dangers that take a very specific form. Barbara Toffler was chief ethics officer at the large accounting firm Arthur Andersen before it collapsed. She has provided a list of career killers for people working in that organization.

EXECUTIVE SUMMARY 10-2

TOFFLER'S LIST OF CAREER KILLERS

- Over-customizing your office
- Not getting results
- Being low energy
- Making yourself unreachable
- Sugar-coating the truth
- Trying to do it all alone

---❖---

Why, we might ask, were these actions considered career killers in the company?

Over-customizing one's office made a person seem to want to stand out in a culture that encouraged selfless devotion to the firm. The firm's culture encouraged hard driving, so getting results was critical to success and not getting them was disastrous. Similarly, the firm's culture insisted on hard work, so having low energy made one stand out in a negative way. Some people in the firm wanted to be able to reach others in the firm for business needs whenever and wherever—so being unreachable was not tolerated. A person at the company had little or no private space in her life. Sugarcoating the truth was a danger because bosses wanted to know what was really going on (a positive characteristic of the firm's culture). Finally, the company emphasized teamwork, so there was no place for the star or for the individual.

The culture of each organization includes such a list, some items reflecting good qualities of the culture, some bad. Ordinarily, an individual cannot pick and choose among these —we are held to each, whether we think it good or bad.

Why Leaders Go Wrong

People work their way to top leadership positions, and suddenly seem to lose their way. From being leaders they turn into something else—self-centered individuals acting for themselves, or pointing in a direction that is unethical or immoral. Some people say that they are still leaders, but bad leaders. What they mean is not that these individuals are ineffective leaders ("bad" meaning ineffective), but rather that they point in the wrong direction ("bad" meaning morally objectionable). (See, for example, Barbara Kellerman, **Bad Leadership: What It Is, How It Happens, Why It Matters,** Boston: Harvard Business School Press, 2004.)

Why do good leaders go bad? The fact is that there is a dark side of leadership, and leaders too often slip into it. Leaders can slip into rigidity, callousness, and corruption, and do so all too often. There are two broad reasons why leaders go wrong.

Leaders give into temptation. Greed, envy, lust, pride, and similar things are common in human beings. Perhaps they are even part of our basic nature, rather than acquired as we watch the conduct of others and make our way through life. Leaders acquire influence with others and control of many things, including large sums of money, the direction of other people, and private knowledge about others. If they convert the objective of their leadership from that of the good of the organization generally (whether it be a nation's government, a business organization, or a not-for-profit entity) to that of themselves and/or their close associates, then they have effectively ceased to be leaders and have instead become exploiters of others. Such former leaders, with their leadership skills intact and their continuing positions of authority, can amass great fortunes, go on ego trips in which they try to outdistance their competitors, use their positions to gain sexual favors, or become strutting celebrities in the popular eye. None of these things are for the benefit of those led; all are for the benefit of the person who used to be a leader and now is merely an exploiter.

Leaders become unsettled by power. Exercising power properly requires great self-discipline (to avoid the temptations identified above) and strength of character. When people who lack either of these characteristics reach positions of power, they often become disoriented. Previously, other people had limited what they could do and say. They had leaders, or bosses, who placed limits on their actions. Now, as they have attained top leadership positions, there is no one in authority to restrain their behavior. They operate with much greater freedom than before.

The Potential for Conflicts of Interest

Conflicts of interest can arise for leaders. For example, a leader won an assignment from the government that involved a great deal of money for the not-for-profit organization for which she worked. She saw an opportunity to make money for herself, and her family, by buying property in the geographical area she was helping to develop as part of her organization's contract. She didn't consider this a conflict of interest, and didn't consider what she was doing illegal. At the same time, she had a friend who was a high official of the government, although not in the agency that granted her contract for the assignment. She offered her friend an opportunity to do some investing as well, and he did.

Soon her friend was offered the position of CEO of the not-for-profit for which she worked. Then auditors in the government became concerned about a possible conflict of interest in her dealings, and insisted that what she had done was illegal. Her friend, now CEO of the not-for-profit, had two options—one to accept the government's position, apologize for the situation, tell his friend that she had to make restitution, and try to get out of the situation. In fact, that's probably what would have happened, except that now the friend was CEO of the not-for-profit. At the friend's fingertips inside the organization were a strong legal department and millions of dollars to call upon for defense against the charges; outside the organization were many friends who had supported the not-for-profit's mission over many years. The friend decided not to settle the matter, but to insist that there was no wrongdoing and to fight the government in court.

The friend had the resources, and no one was in a position to tell him not to do it. He was the leader of the organization; he had the key position of authority. So he took the organization to court, where it lost in a trial. Even then, the friend wasn't done. He had the public relations office denounce the jury verdict as wrongheaded and sought other forums in which to fight the government's claims.

Meanwhile the reputation of the organization he now headed was being damaged by the positions he was taking. But the friend was in control and could pursue his course until the board of trustees that had picked her for the position decided that he had to be reversed on this matter, or even had to leave his position. Power made a wrong course of action possible.

A Question of Ethics

Jack had founded a clothing company and helped it grow into a very large and successful firm. He and his name became closely associated with its product: His name was the brand name and the company's name. The press was continually writing feature stories about him, which his public relations office had planted, and which were almost always laudatory. He was used to having his way.

Jack grew very rich. He had many acquaintances, among them people who had founded their own companies, and he began to get opportunities to invest his fortune in a variety of profitable ways. He bought stock in new companies and watched it soar in value. One day, he and a friend were en route to a vacation hideaway on his company's private jet when his cell phone rang. It was Jack's stockbroker. The broker had heard that the CEO of another firm (who was a personal friend of Jack's) was selling his stock fast. It was possible that the stock was about to take a big fall. Jack owned some of the stock. He ordered his broker to sell it. A few days later bad news about the company hit the media and the stock price of the company collapsed. Jack's timely stock sale had saved him an amount of money that was not much to him, but to most people would have been a sizable sum.

There are laws to prevent people who have advance information about a company in which the public can own stock from trading on their own benefit in that stock (the insider trading laws). Jack's friend who was CEO of the other company had done exactly that. He was in deep legal trouble. As federal investigators looked into trading in the stock prior to the bad news becoming public, they discovered Jack's trades. They decided that Jack might have violated the insider trading laws and made a visit to his office to discuss the matter.

Jack was convinced that what he'd done wasn't in violation of the law. In his view, he wasn't an insider. He wasn't an employee of the other company; he wasn't a director of the other company; how could he be an insider? He was, to his own mind, simply an investor selling stock on the basis of a tip from his broker.

Jack's Response

Jack was irritated that the federal agents would waste his time with this matter; he was irritated that they suspected him of wrongdoing. He could have simply explained what had happened; that he didn't think he had violated any laws; but that if the federal government had another view, then he was sorry about the misunderstanding. He'd apologize and give the money back.

Millions of people trade billions of shares of stock each day. Insider trading is prohibited, but people often disagree on whether or not a trade was legal. Jack's situation was uncertain at best; a court might find him guilty of insider trading, and it might not. It wasn't a big thing if he handled it correctly.

It was rather like a speeding ticket. Motorists speed all the time. Police officers watch the roads. They stop some people for speeding, otherwise the laws would be completely ignored. But most violators are not stopped at all. So when a person is stopped for speeding, in a way it can be seen as somewhat unfair. Why me and not the next motorist? But there are differences in attitude about being stopped. Some people just say, "Officer, I'm sorry if I was speeding. I didn't think I was, but I might have been distracted, and didn't realize it. I won't do it again."

Career Hurdles We Create

Most police officers hearing this would say, "Well, don't do it again." Or they'd say, "I'll give you a warning ticket, but don't do it again." Or they'd say, "I still have to give you a ticket." Then the driver would take the ticket and pay it.

But, sometimes a driver takes a different approach when the police officer stops him, saying, "Why did you stop me? I wasn't speeding? Why are you picking on me? See all those other people speeding—why aren't you out there catching them?" Or even adds, "Why are you stopping me for speeding; why aren't you chasing murders or terrorists or something?"

Most police officers hearing this would not only write out a ticket but might even take the driver to jail.

Irritated at being questioned by the federal agents about possible insider trading, Jack essentially took the second approach. "I did nothing wrong," he said. "Why are you bothering me? Why aren't you out after the CEOs who have stolen billions from shareholders at Enron and WorldCom?"

Angered, the federal investigators pressed the case.

Jack was a powerful person. He didn't like being pressed. He told people who worked for him to clean up the records of his phone conversations with his broker; he told his lawyers to get the federal agents off his back; when the investigation became public, he told his press spokesman to say that the feds were simply persecuting him largely because he was a successful entrepreneur.

Jack wouldn't have done any of these things if he weren't a powerful person in a position of leadership. The more he criticized the federal agents and insisted on his innocence, the

231

more they thought they had to pursue the matter to show that they were enforcing the law and couldn't just be pushed away.

Jack went to court, to a jury trial. He lost. He went to jail for a brief time. His company's sales declined; consequently its stock price dropped significantly. The chairman of the board of his company, whom Jack had recruited with great personal effort, resigned.

Jack had become confused. He'd thought that because he was successful and powerful in his company, he couldn't be challenged successfully. Pride had become arrogance, and he paid a very big price for it, financially and in terms of his personal reputation as well as his company's reputation.

Leadership, Responsibility and Accountability

One of the most frequently identified characteristics of leadership is that it is lonely at the top. In reality, this is only partly true. Actually, it's not lonely at all: There are dozens of people, sometimes hundreds, who crowd about the leader, flattering her or him, trying to get the leader's attention focused on their own efforts to obtain jobs, contracts, pay increases, promotions, work for their friends and relatives—favor after favor in an almost endless list.

Where the leader is without company is in the responsibility for difficult choices and decisions. There are many who will advise her or him, but none who bear final accountability for the result. Ultimately, responsibility and accountability belong to the leader alone.

One of the most dramatic examples in history of the loneliness of the leader involves General Robert E. Lee, the top military officer of the Confederacy during the American Civil War.

Lee sat astride his horse on the third day of the battle of Gettysburg as the survivors of the disastrous charge of Pickett's division against the Union Army straggled back to the Confederate lines, most of their comrades lying dead and wounded behind them. To his defeated and disillusioned troops, Lee repeated again and again, "It's all my fault!"

Great leaders remind themselves continually that the responsibility is theirs alone, and that they must defend themselves continually against people who will flatter and mislead them in pursuit of personal agendas.

Marcus Aurelius was emperor of Rome at the height of its power (during the middle of the second century AD). He struggled continually to keep a proper perspective on life and his leadership role, putting down his thoughts in a book we know as his **Meditations**. Among the things he told himself are:

- "Men despise and flatter one another; and men wish to raise themselves above one another, and crouch before one another."

- "It should make no difference to you if you are warm or cold, if you are doing your duty."

- "Don't let yourself be made into a Caesar…keep yourself simple, good, pure, serious, free from affectation, a friend of justice…."

Given great power, leaders begin to exercise it for their personal benefit, and don't realize this is what they are doing. It becomes possible for them to associate only with people who flatter them and tell them that they are brilliant. It's difficult for the leader to recognize, sometimes, that these things are not actually true, but are being said in hopes of obtaining an advantage for the flatterer.

The Dangers of Flattery

Many leaders are misled by flattery. A man became CEO of one of the largest firms in the U.S. In a few years he proved himself a very effective business leader. He repositioned the company and made billions of dollars for shareholders. He became the darling of the business media. He had a large staff inside the company who were increasingly flattering to him.

A presidential election was looming on the horizon. As always, there was criticism in the business community of what it considered wrong-headed political leadership in Washington. "Tom," his close advisors in the company began to tell him, "why shouldn't you run for president? What this country needs now is a strong business executive to lead it. Everyone would support you!"

Tom should have known better. He'd never been in politics in his life. He was not particularly handsome or charismatic, not a warm or caring personality; he knew almost nothing about many public issues—but he disregarded all this. He found it easy to believe that he had a unique leadership talent and that his country needed him; his closest advisors were encouraging him to think in those terms.

The first presidential primary elections for the two major U.S. political parties take place in New Hampshire in February of the election year. In the months prior to February there is a continual parade of politicians to New Hampshire to speak to local audiences to test their likelihood of success in the upcoming primaries. Tom's staff persuaded him to make the pilgrimage in spring, summer, and fall of the year preceding the election to New Hampshire to give speeches. He made several trips; he allowed his speeches to be publicized in the newspaper. Quietly, he began to position himself as a presidential candidate and to use his staff as a campaign staff to prepare for a possible run.

But he was out of his comfort zone in politics. Within the company he was decisive, strong, gave clear direction, was certain of his opinions, impatient with criticism. None of these personal characteristics translated well into the political arena.

Decisiveness seemed opinionated; strength seemed uncaring; clear direction seemed naiveté; certainty seemed misplaced among the ambiguities of public issues; impatience with criticism seemed arrogance. Tom gave four major speeches in New Hampshire, saw in his audiences' reactions that he was not being well received, and moved to shut down his campaign. He told his staff to dispose of all evidence that he had ever considered a political career.

When reporters asked about it, he denied that he'd ever had any interest in politics whatever; he said that he'd visited New Hampshire only on behalf of his company and only for commercial reasons. He put the embarrassment behind him and never again let flatterers deflect him from his focus on the success of the corporation he headed.

It had been a close thing. Even when his speeches were being poorly received by New Hampshire voters, his staff had urged him to continue his political effort, saying that the voters were dumb, and that the speeches could be improved. Tom was still the nation's best hope for a great president, they insisted.

He could have kept on that course, becoming an announced candidate, and then he would have been humiliated publicly in the primary election. He could have gone very wrong. It was due to the influence of flatterers, he recognized, and he held himself fortunate to have seen through them as soon as he had.

Making Transitions in Our Careers

It is easy to trip over ourselves when a major transition looms in our careers. There are two general types of errors we can make:

- Being afraid to make a necessary transition.
- Bungling a transition if we try it.

How can we minimize the danger of either type of mistake?

To avoid being afraid to make a necessary transition, we have to keep a continual inventory of our strengths. They should be increasing. If we go a year or so without adding to the list of our abilities—whether in specific skills, experience or personal competencies— then we're no longer growing in our position, and we really should start looking for another assignment. As we contemplate possible moves, we need to see beyond our current role, in terms of both industry and job function.

We're likely to need some help to assess ourselves and our progress, or lack thereof. It's useful to think of ourselves as if we're a business of one, and to try to put together a personal board of directors. It's probably best not to give our support team the label of a personal board, but that's how we might think of them.

Our purpose is similar to the purpose of a CEO with his or her company's board of directors—it is oversight of progress and problems. We want to know what the members of our board think of us honestly, where we are headed, and if we need to make a transition.

Who should make up the board? Probably a few people from work who know us well, for example, a mentor if we have one and a close coworker or two. In some instances our boss might be in the group, though this is not common because a boss often may have a personal interest in keeping us in her department.

A family member belongs in the group (perhaps a spouse if we have one, or a close brother or sister, or even a parent), and one or two close friends—ideally one of our own age and another who is older and more experienced. Our purpose is to assemble a group that will try to be objective about our current situation and our prospects.

Working with our personal board of directors (probably in one-on-ones rather than in a meeting of the group), we need to identify our passions—what gets our juices going. It isn't a silly question to ask someone who knows us well, "What do you think I really care about?" As humans we are so inclined to illusion and self-deception, not always for selfish reasons, but just because objectivity is difficult, that it can be very enlightening to see how others assess even our inner motives.

When we know what excites us, we can start to hunt for it in a particular position. We need to work out the specifics of what we want to achieve in the new position. It is very important that we don't bungle a career transition by moving into a new position that is wrong for us. When we do, we may want to go back where we came from, but that can be very chancy.

Then it's time for research, to identify possible options in a fact-based way. We're moving from hope toward reality.

Finally, we should write down a plan for our job search. We should circulate it among our personal board of directors, refine it on the basis of their comments, and then implement it. If we've been able to involve people close to us at work in developing our personal job strategy, then if we decide to leave, hopefully they will understand and support our decision. We don't want to burn any bridges if we can help it.

EXECUTIVE SUMMARY 10-3

HOW TO DECIDE ON A CAREER TRANSITION AND ACCOMPLISH IT

1. Find your strengths; see beyond your current functional or industry role.
2. Build your personal board of directors.
3. Identify what gets your juices going.
4. Identify what you would like to achieve in the new position.
5. Generate options from fact-based research on desired positions.
6. Develop a written plan that supports your job strategy.
7. Obtain assistance from your personal board of directors or from job placement professionals in accomplishing your transition.

Adapted from "The Spencer Stuart Job Survival Guide" (from James M. Citrin and Richard A. Smith, **The Five Patterns of Extraordinary Careers,** New York: Random House, 2003, pp. 235-40.)

Burning or Building Bridges?

Emilio graduated from business school and took a job in a manufacturing company that had a hot new computer product and appeared to have a great future. He started as a foreman and worked his way off the production floor into a higher management position. He was recognized as a rising star, but then the company missed a change in technology and began to fail.

Emilio looked around and found a job at a similar level at another high-tech firm. Five years later, the same thing occurred. Emilio gave up on high tech because it seemed too risky, and took a job in an industry that saw fewer rapid and dramatic changes in products. There he continued to advance. Soon he was a vice president in charge of all operations for the firm in Latin America. He was looking at a chance for the top job. Then another manager was selected for CEO and at almost the same moment, Emilio got an offer from another firm in the same industry. The firm was larger, the pay better, and Emilio thought he might reach the top there. So he went to the new firm, but he was careful to leave on a friendly basis. Soon after he arrived at the new firm, Emilio discovered that things were not as they had been represented to him. The company was in deep financial trouble; the promises made to Emilio were not going to be kept.

Emilio and his boss from the old company had kept in touch, and sometimes had lunch together. When his old boss said that he missed Emilio at the firm, Emilio saw his chance. He said, "I miss being there too." His old boss picked up on the opening. "Would you come back?" he asked. "I might," Emilio said. "What would it take to get you back?" his old boss inquired. Emilio decided to be modest—not to pretend that things were great at his new company and ask for a raise over that high level. "Just a little more than I was making when I left," Emilio replied.

A week later Emilio had an offer from his old company at the same position he'd left. He took it. A year later he was given more responsibility, now managing all international activities except the Far East. He was even back on a possible route to the CEO's chair.

Emilio had been fortunate. Because he had not shown any anger or disappointment when he was passed over for the top job, and left on good terms with his boss, he was able to quickly correct the mistake he'd made in taking a job at the new company.

Nonetheless, it is important for us to realize how unusual Emilio's experience is. Generally, when a person leaves a department or a firm, it occasions considerable bitterness among the people he or she has left. The only common exceptions to this are when a person is forced to leave by a downsizing or the sale of the unit in which the person works. But when someone leaves looking for a promotion, salary increase, or better opportunities, some level of resentment is the usual response.

Even people who use an inter-company job posting system to find a position in a different department in the same company often get treated like deserters. People in the department being left feel a sense of betrayal, even though the person leaving has an explanation for why he or she is doing it. Often a relationship of trust between those remaining and a person who has left cannot be re-established.

Even when a person does return, as Emilio did, generally the transition is unpleasant and difficult. A person who left to go to a competitor, for example, and then is recruited back by top management, is still likely to encounter a significant amount of resentment by coworkers who had not been part of the decision to take him or her back. The returnee is likely to be forced to do such things as make a firm-wide presentation on his/her experience at the competitor; he can expect to be continually barraged with questions about his loyalty to the firm. In the end, it is possible to win back a reputation for loyalty by performing well, but for a period of a year or more, the returnee is likely to be pressured in a variety of ways to prove himself and his loyalty again.

How Relationships Matter

The difficulties of returning to a previous employer can be minimized if we have built strong personal relationships with the extended team at the company we left previously, and showed a high degree of openness and honesty about why we left. If we've built a strong relationship with our superiors in a company, then we may be able to comfortably discuss with them our upcoming career plans. Then if we go to another firm to get experience not available where we were, or go off to business school for further development, we may be able to rejoin the company without hard feelings from superiors. Yet there is still likely to be resentment among our peers.

Each of us can be disappointed that we didn't get a key promotion, and make a mistake about where we go next, but only the smartest of us will have maintained good relations where we'd been, and, if need be, could return and start back up the ladder again.

Leadership: How to Lead, How to Live

CHAPTER REFERENCES:

Citrin, James M. and Richard A. Smith. **The Five Patterns of Extraordinary Careers.** New York: Random House, 2003.

Kellerman, Barbara. **Bad Leadership: What It Is, How It Happens, Why It Matters.** Boston: Harvard Business School Press, 2004.

Lichtenberg, Ronna. **It's Not Business, It's Personal: The 9 Relationship Principles that Power Your Career.** New York: Hyperion, 2001.

Toffler, Barbara Lee. **Final Accounting: Ambition, Greed and the Fall of Arthur Andersen.** New York: Random House, 2003.

ADDITIONAL READINGS:

Bolles, Richard Nelson. **What Color Is Your Parachute? 2005: A Practical Manual for Job-Hunters and Career-Changers.** Berkeley, CA: Ten Speed Press, 2005.

Grove, Andrew S. **Only the Paranoid Survive.** New York: Currency, 1996.

Leadership: How to Lead, How to Live

Chapter 11

Leading a Team

It is better to lead from behind and to put others in front, especially when you celebrate victory when nice things occur. You take the front line when there is danger. Then people will appreciate your leadership.

- Nelson Mandela, South African statesman

Early in our careers, the most likely opportunity for many of us to exercise leadership in a significant way is as a team leader. If such an opportunity arises, we should recognize it as a major chance to develop and exhibit our leadership skills.

There are many types of teams, but two especially merit identification here:

- The first is a group in which people do specialized tasks under the direction of a manager who is labeled a team leader and who herself receives direction from a department manager outside the team. There is little practical difference between this structure and a normal hierarchical business unit; it is a team in name only. The role of the person labeled team leader is essentially an administrative one, communicating directions from higher ups, using rewards and punishments to motivate people, assigning tasks to individuals, assessing their performance and bearing responsibility to his or her boss for the results of the group's activities. This sort of team operates primarily under traditional managerial authority.

- The second is group of people who do specialized tasks, but also have general responsibilities for the overall mission of the team under the leadership (not direction) of a team leader. The people in this type of team are empowered to act in pursuit of its mission with others as necessary and appropriate to accomplish the mission. This is a more substantial team. The leader doesn't bear a manager's sole responsibility for the team's results, but instead joins with the team members in responsibility for results.

Leading a Team

Also, the leader exercises to a much lesser degree the administrative and directive functions of a manager.

The second sort of team, the *empowered team*, is of greater interest to us because if offers a greater opportunity for leadership skill development and demonstration.

The Role of Leaders in Empowered Teams

The leader in an empowered team does not direct the work. (Please see Executive Summary 11-1 for a summary of his or her responsibilities). In fact, he or she may participate as an individual contributor within the team as well as acting as team leader.

EXECUTIVE SUMMARY 11-1

LEADER'S ROLE IN EMPOWERED TEAM

A leader in an empowered team is responsible for:

- Making sure the team can reach decisions in a timely and effective fashion.

- Making sure that the team communicates well internally and externally.

- Being sure that the team can resolve internal conflicts.

- Making sure that the team remains committed to its mission.

———————❖———————

What is most important to us to recognize is that it is not the responsibility of the team leader to do things for the team, or even to assist it in doing things. It is not the responsibility of the team leader, for example, to help the team make decisions, or to enhance its communications skills, or to help it resolve internal conflicts, or to help keep it committed to its mission.

Instead, the team leader's responsibility is to see that these things are happening—effective and timely decision-making; good communications; resolution of possible conflicts between team members; a continuing commitment by all team members to the mission of the team. When the team leader notices something amiss, then he should seek support in getting it fixed, or if he can, help himself. But his primary responsibility is not helping, it is to see that the matter gets fixed or resolved.

Ultimately, making decisions is the team's role; effective communications is the team's responsibility; resolving internal conflicts is what team members must do; and the team must motivate itself to continuing commitment to its mission. The team leader's responsibility is to see that all of these things are happening, and if they are not, then to call the team's attention to the shortfall, and to work with the team to get it corrected. If the team leader can be a resource in this effort, that is fine, but he may also be a catalyst for the team resolving the difficulty or may help bring in outside counselors to help.

Let us review key responsibilities of the team and its leader:

- **Decision-making:** It is not the responsibility of the team leader to make decisions for the team—decision-making is a responsibility of the team. The leader's function is to be sure that the team makes decisions well.

- **Task assignments:** It is not the responsibility of the team leader to give directions to team members as to what work to do; deciding who in the team is to do what in achieving the mission must remain the responsibility of the team.

- **Conflict resolution:** It is not the team leader's responsibility to resolve conflicts that may arise among the members of the team; it is the team leader's responsibility to see that few conflicts arise and that those that do are resolved effectively by the team.

- **Communications:** It is not the team leader's responsibility to communicate with each member of the team about his or her work, nor with outside units of the overall organization about the team's work; instead, it is the team leader's responsibility to be sure that there are effective communications among the members of the team so that work gets done properly and on time, and that the team communicates in an effective way with other parts of the organization.

- **Commitment to the team's mission:** It is not the responsibility of the team leader to see that all members of the team remain committed to its mission; it is the responsibility of the team to motivate itself and to exhibit commitment to its mission; it is the clear responsibility of the team leader to see that this is happening successfully in the team and if it is not, to initiate a corrective effort in the team.

In general, it is the responsibility of the team leader to see that the internal processes of the team—decision-making, communications, conflict resolution—are working well so that the team functions well, and that team members remain committed. The last means that the team leader must by example and inspiration help keep morale high in the team and commitment high to its mission. The team leader ordinarily lacks the motivation tools (rewards and penalties) of the manager, and must rely on leadership skills alone.

A specific duty of the team member is to conduct the meetings of the team. This is a most important function because most teams make decisions of all types within team meetings. What work is to be done, who is to do it, and who is responsible for the outcome are all decisions of an empowered team—not of its leader. The team leader's role is to run meetings that make these decisions properly and in a timely fashion.

The Challenges of Team Meetings

This is not easy to do. Meetings tend to generate into either endless talking sessions or bitter controversies. In the first instance, the harder working team members soon grow bored and irritated at what they perceive to be the loss of productive time in a meeting, and they cease to attend, or if they attend, they cease to participate actively. They sit at the meeting thinking about other things than the meeting's agenda and even doing other things. Inexperienced team leaders grow angry with them.

But the problem is in the meeting, not with the team members. It is the team leader's role to see that meetings don't become mere bull sessions that alienate the best people in the team.

Alternatively, meetings can become occasions for deep frustration occasioned by bitter divisions among team members over key decisions the team must make. Such divisions often degenerate

Leading a Team

into personal animosities that make effective teamwork impossible.

It is the responsibility of the team leader to see that this does not happen. When he or she perceives that divisions of opinion are not getting resolved and that personal animosities are developing, he must get the people together to resolve the problems, or, in the extreme, recommend to higher level management that the team be dissolved or members of the team replaced.

A Checklist for Team Leaders

Here is a basic checklist for team leaders, covering the key areas of responsibility.

1. Make sure that management has put in place the necessary conditions for team effectiveness, including:

   - A fully understandable mandate for what the team is to do.

   - A clear and explicit specification of the deliverables of the team—the specific things for which it is responsible.

   - Appropriate staffing, especially that all the skills needed to accomplish the mission are included in the group of people assigned to the team or are available from the outside on an as-needed basis.

2. Facilitate communication within the team by:

   - Tracking the participation, style and listening skill of each team member.

   - Being sure team members address ideas advanced by each other rather than attacking each other for those ideas.

   - Being sure all members of the team are trained in giving and receiving constructive criticism. This is especially important.

CONSTRUCTIVE CRITICISM

Constructive criticism is an important skill in itself, involving giving criticism in a way that doesn't offend the other person, and receiving it with an attitude of trying to resolve a problem rather than resisting a personal attack.

It is the leader's responsibility to see that team leaders are trained in this skill and are able to implement it properly. Otherwise, a team will either avoid candid discussion of problems for fear that team members will take offense at criticism, or cause team meetings to degenerate into name-calling and overt personal conflict.

An example of non-constructive criticism:

Susan says: Tom, you really blew that setup yesterday.

An example of constructive criticism:

Susan says: Tom, I had trouble working with the set-up you left yesterday; can we review how it's done?

An example of non-constructive response to criticism:

Tom says: Susan, why are you on my back? Are you so perfect yourself? Remember how you messed up that customer meeting two days ago?

An example of constructive response to criticism:

Tom says: Susan, I thought I'd done that right. What was the problem? How can we fix matters?

3. Insure a rigorous decision-making process within the team by:

- Thoroughly framing, examining and identifying each issue which is submitted to the team for decision.

- Making the decision-making process explicit.

- Holding decision-making within a proper time frame so that it works in a timely fashion.

- Insuring that the leader doesn't make the decisions, but exercises her influence to see that the decision-process is effective and on time.

4. Encourage development of appropriate norms and rules of interpersonal interaction by:

- Encouraging collaboration and constructive discussion.

- Treating mistakes as a source of learning rather than a reason to punish.

- Helping team members understand how their personal team roles differ from their roles as individual contributors or managers within a hierarchy.

5. Manage the team's context by:

- Procuring resources needed by the team for success.

- Interacting with suppliers to the team and customers of the team (internal to the organization or external) on behalf of the team.

- Defending the team against unwarranted criticism from elsewhere in the organization (there is no unwarranted criticism from a customer outside the organization—there are only misunderstandings to be cleared up—as the external customer is presumed always right).

Leadership in a Team

In Chapter 3 we identified seven bases for leadership. As a team leader, we must have at least one basis upon which other team members will accept our leadership. If we've been appointed team leader by upper management, then that formal authority can serve as an initial basis. It will not last long, however, if we do not show that we have the skills to lead the team properly.

Expertise regarding how to lead a team will serve as a solid basis for leadership; but so will expertise with respect to the mission of the team, or commitment to its mission. Other potential bases such as empathy or values are less likely to be effective in the small group atmosphere of a team than they are in a broader context. While charisma is always a solid basis for leadership, in a team setting it must be accompanied by skill in the responsibilities of a team leader. If it is not, charisma becomes merely an occasion for team members to regret that someone who seems so likely to be a leader is not one at all.

Applying the Key Qualities in a Team Setting

What key qualities of leadership are important for a team leader? All but one of the key qualities of leadership are important to a team leader. The one that is not important is decisiveness—because decision-making and individual action are not part of the role of a team leader. Decisiveness is a

Leading a Team

desired quality of the team; action taking is a desired quality of the team. The team leader needs to use the other key qualities of leadership we have identified—including passion, integrity, adaptability, conviction, self-knowledge, humility, emotional toughness and emotional resonance—to lead the team to successful decision-making and action taking.

Applying the Central Skills in a Team Setting

How are the central skills of leadership employed by a team leader?

- **Defining a leader's vision.** The vision of a team leader should be about the successful internal operation of the team, rather than about how it accomplishes its mission. The mission-related vision should be that of the team as a whole; its leader's vision should include that the team have a compelling vision of its mission. The team leader's vision should also include team members communicating effectively with one another; engaging in constructive criticism and avoiding internal dissension; and every team member being a significant contributor to the team's mission.

- **Setting an example.** In many ways the team leader should provide a model for team members—of how to communicate effectively, of giving and receiving constructive criticism; of identifying and solving problems; of commitment to the mission, etc.

- **Inspiring others.** By his devotion to his role, by commitment to the team's mission, by respect for each member of the team, the team leader can inspire others to similar behavior.

- **Seeing previously unrecognized potential in others.** Empowered teams lack narrowly defined job assignments and therefore provide a wide range for team members to expand their contribution. In this setting, therefore, a team leader is given maximum opportunity to exercise the central leadership skill of seeing previously unrecognized potential in other people. From the moment of the team's formation the leader should be carefully observing team members with the intention of encouraging each one to expand his or her scope of activities; creating a "culture of reach" within the team in which each person strives to learn and do more.

- **Establishing a supportive organizational culture.** This final central leadership skill is the most important one for the leader of an empowered team. It is his or her principle responsibility. Everything he or she does as team leader is intended to establish a supportive climate within the team for its pursuit of its mission. All other leadership skills are exercised to this single purpose.

Appropriate Leadership Styles in a Team Setting

What styles of leadership are appropriate for the leader of an empowered team? It should be readily apparent that several of the styles of leadership are not suitable for a team leader.

- The commanding style of leadership is not suitable because the team leader is not the decision-maker; the team makes decisions. Decisiveness is therefore misplaced in a team leader.

- The important vision is that of the team about its mission; the vision of the team leader must remain a more modest one—it is about the effective operation of the team. It is not focused on distant achievements or rewards. Hence, visionary leadership is out of place for a team leader.

- Authentic leadership via ethics and fair-dealing is very much appropriate in a team context. In fact, in the small circle of people that compose most teams, it is not only essential but also urgently required. Unethical behavior by a leader is quickly perceived and is usually very demoralizing to the team. Fair dealing is crucial because the team leader is in continual interaction with most members of the team and is usually observed by many team members in his or her dealings with other team members. Unfair dealing are recognized and resented by members of the team, creating tensions in the team and undermining the cooperative relationship that is a key to team success.

- The supportive style of leadership is fully appropriate and desired for a team leader. His role is to support the team and its members. The better he is at it, the better the team will perform.

- The demagogic style of leadership is completely inappropriate and will be ineffective within the small human circle of a team. It will make the leader appear ridiculous and will cause him to become a subject of contempt, raising the question of whether the team will be able to function properly.

Employing Leadership Abilities in a Team Setting

Each of the key abilities of leadership has a major contribution to make to the success of a team leader.

- **Ability to energize others.** Part of the team leader's responsibility is to help keep the team excited about its mission and to see that each member of the team is energized to contribute as much as he or she can. In this aspect of her responsibility the team leader is much like the coach of a sports team. The coach doesn't play the game. He or she has to see that those who do play are energized to play hard and well. The team leader is usually a player as well, unlike a coach in sports, but needs to be energizing the other players.

    In sports a team captain often serves this role; but has a coach on the sidelines as well. The team leader has no coach to turn to, and instead must serve and player and coach at once. It is therefore a very challenging role, and a great place to learn leadership skills and abilities of almost all types. Often energizing others can be best accomplished by a combination of personal contact (monitoring attitude, helping identify and fully resolve any potentially demoralizing concerns, encouraging, complimenting on success, helping when frustration arises) and displaying one's own commitment to the mission, and energy about its accomplishment. It is a combination of support and example by the leader that energizes others.

- **Ability to communicate clearly.** It is a key aspect of the team leader's role that she conducts the meetings of the team. In that aspect of her role, she must be able to communicate clearly with all team members. We say communicate with, rather than to, because as we see in the next point, listening clearly is as important an element of clear communication as is speaking.

- **Ability to listen effectively.** Listening may be the most important part of communication for a team leader. It is crucial that the team leader be responding to what people are asking, not what he thinks they are asking or should be asking. The team leader is not the boss—he is not giving directions; he is trying to keep a team on track, getting it to make informed and timely decisions. He must see that task assignments are clearly given, understood and accepted, and that team morale is kept high. His job is to respond, not to set the agenda—as such he has to hear clearly what the team needs. A team leader, who does not or will not listen carefully, even if she talks clearly, will be ineffective because she isn't likely to be responding to team members in a productive way.

- **Ability to earn respect and confidence from others.** Team members will accept a number of different bases for the leadership of the team leader at the outset of the team's existence. But very quickly, in the relatively small and intimate circle of a team, what will matter most is the effectiveness of the team leader, and her ability (by demonstrating leadership abilities and skills) to earn the respect and confidence of team members—not as an individual personality or as an individual contributor in the team, but as its leader.

Should a person who is team leader fail to demonstrate the leadership skills and abilities necessary to help the team function effectively, he will not earn respect and confidence, his leadership base will disappear, and he will be ineffectual. The team will then seek another leader, or will itself fail. As this is not the outcome that a person seeking higher leadership opportunities via success as a team leader wants to have, it is vitally important for a leader to gain the trust and respect of an empowered team.

Leading A Team

Sometimes when accept leadership of a team, we discover that the challenges we face are different than those we anticipated.

> "I became President of a not-for-profit organization. We have 150 employees, a big budget and I was approached because of my business background to be President. I thought long and hard—I really had no interest in taking on any leadership role outside my business—but eventually I accepted because I believed in the ideals of this club and thought I could take it to a higher plain.
>
> The first few weeks were OK—I had 20 people ask to be VP and I went for six joint VPs to spread to work around so that no-one felt overwhelmed. I also thought that if people wanted to help I should find away to let them. I let them choose their specific roles.
>
> What I didn't allow for was bickering between VPs as to who was putting the most effort in, who should book which function and who was "resume padding" and who wasn't.
>
> I had a lot going on and couldn't give the club much attention, and the bickering became worse. I couldn't believe how petty the controversies became. It was

affecting my work—I'd spend hours addressing personal issues among the team rather than working.

I really thought of just walking away; but I had a long talk with my brother who reminded me that the reason I took the job was still there and I was letting trivial issues bother me. But, he warned me, as long as I let the situation drift it was probably going to get worse.

I decided not to directly address the bickering, nor to complain about it to the VPs. I called a meeting and said, "We are re-organizing and changing the budget—there will be a lot coming up. Who can help? If you are busy say no. Please just don't promise to do something if you haven't the time. The club is going really well but now we need to step it up a notch." From among the volunteers, I chose who did what.

Just that hint of leadership from me and the in-fighting stopped. I had placed myself above it all. Once I had given that talk, and treated all the VPs equally, my relationships changed with them. Those who had thought they had a special "in" with me were angry. I had to give up trying to be closer friends with some than others. But the club works better now and I'm getting more work done."

The responsibilities of leadership can be unnerving. Sometimes a leader even becomes a scapegoat. A young man had assumed a leadership role in his organization when the top executive made a decision without consulting him (as is common). The young man had to deliver the news to his department; everyone blamed him for the outcome even though he had no control over the matter. He felt ostracized because of that.

Leadership: How to Lead, How to Live

CHAPTER REFERENCES:

Hackman, J. Richard. **Leading Teams: Setting the Stage for Great Performances**. Boston: Harvard Business School Press, 2002.

Katzenbach, Jon R. **The Wisdom of Teams**. New York: HarperBusiness, 2003.

ADDITIONAL READINGS:

Fisher, Kimball. **Leading Self-Directed Work Teams**. New York: McGraw-Hill, 2000.

Leadership: How to Lead, How to Live

Chapter 12

Leadership in the Midst of External Change

We must become the change we want to see.

- Mahatma Gandhi, Indian independence leader

Leadership: How to Lead, How to Live

Ours is a time of rapid and dynamic change in the context of our organizations. This poses special risks and opportunities for leaders, and for those who aspire to leadership. What are the key changes that are occurring and how should leaders address them? We turn to these questions in this chapter.

Leadership in the Midst of External Change

The Challenge of the New Economy

A very different economy, a new economy, is evolving rapidly in our world. Globalization and electronic communications (including the Internet) are coupling to create the economy of the future. Globalization brings new companies and new workers into every nation's marketplace, and wide-spread electronic networking provides close communications so that orders can be placed and work done at enormous distances.

Organizations must change how they conduct their activities to remain successful. Firms have to compete in the marketplace with other companies that can often bring much lower costs. To compete, our firms have to go to the same sources for production and labor that their new competitors do, or they must rapidly increase productivity in order to cut costs at home.

Even not-for-profits are impacted since if their costs become too high, or if they do not serve their mission on a broad enough scale, other organizations will step in and displace them. In the past it made little since to talk of competition among not-for-profits—now there is great competition. Not-for-profit hospitals, for example, compete for patients with other not-for-profit hospitals, but also with for-profit hospitals and with doctor-run clinics. For many not-for-profits, hiding from the changing global marketplace is no more an option than it is for commercial firms.

The challenge to leadership is dramatic. The effective leader must be prepared continuously for bad news from rapid developments in the global economy. The emergence of new, low-cost competitors from abroad may suddenly cause key customers to leave his firm; the sudden emergence of a new technological advance may make his company's products obsolete overnight.

The cost of a key input (like aviation fuel to an airline) may unexpectedly skyrocket, undermining the profitability of his firm.

Unless a leader has the right organization and people, he and his planners won't have access to the information about key threats and emerging opportunities in the new economy—and his organization's strategy process will be blind. If that should happen, ambitious, impatient people in his organization will demand from the leader a strategy that will keep them excited and give them earning opportunities; otherwise they will race to competitors who offer better prospects.

As important, but much less widely recognized, is that the new economy offers not just threats, but opportunities. Perhaps the opportunities are even greater than the threats. But most leaders focus on the threats, leaving it to a few far-sighted entrepreneurs to pursue the opportunities. Technological advances in many fields, and electronic networking of the world, promise vastly favorable new business economics. Unfortunately, most contemporary business organizations seem incapable of exploiting what technology and global scope are making possible. This is a failure of leadership in our organizations on a large scale.

With more and more efficient communications, it becomes harder, not easier, for an organization to get noticed. So many other organizations are now competing for the attention of customers or clients. The brands of both for-profit firms and not-for-profits can be forgotten or damaged by bad publicity more quickly than ever before. The cost of launching a new brand has become much higher than ever before. It is the responsibility of a leader to find ways to attract attention to his organization's products and services at something other than prohibitive cost.

Mastering an Organization's Changing Environment

When the economic environment is changing so quickly, it remains the responsibility of a leader to insure that her organization masters its environment. This involves three crucial activities:

- Thinking strategically
- Satisfying customers
- Improving company performance

Thinking strategically requires clear analysis and imaginative solutions about:

- The market space
- The organization
- The company's culture
- The speed of reaction and response

The notion is that markets now exist not in places alone, but in cyber space as well, so that the analysis and response must encompass what can be called the *marketspace*, not only the marketplace. Strategic thinking about organization's structure in other terms than shifting lines and boxes and reporting relationships is uncommon, yet new types of organizations are emerging steadily.

It is probably fair to say that in every marketspace there will soon be competitors offering as their competitive advantage higher quality and lower costs derived from their innovative organization arrangements. These innovations include networked organizations, empowered teams, and boundary-less organizations, among others.

Organizational cultures are notoriously resistant to change, but change they must in today's environment, requiring leaders to address issues of corporate culture in a strategic manner.

Finally, for large and well-established organizations speed of reaction and response has never been particularly necessary; but today it is becoming more important. Increasing speed means reducing bureaucracy in large organizations, something much easier to discuss than to actually do. Only in times of severe economic distress do large organizations reduce levels of administration—but in today's environment, organizations that are unable or unwilling to de-bureaucratize are likely to drive themselves into severe economic distress.

The Danger of Strategic Myopia

There is a strategic myopia that seems to affect many leaders. They presume that success is a static situation for which the best strategy is to extend the status quo; yet the new economy is more dynamic and emergent than in the past. The result is that their response to change is not proactive, but instead reactive and reluctant. Few advantages follow from that.

Another element of the myopia is that leaders cannot see the competitive advantages in the combination of various products and production methods that is made possible by acquisitions and divestitures. In effect, strategy for a large organization is a form of asset management. Yet increasingly it matters less what a company owns than how quickly and effectively it exploits what it has. Thus competitive advantages are execution-related rather than asset-based. Only recently has effectiveness of execution found its way into discussion of organizational strategy. Few leaders have exploited the potential in improved execution.

Finally, much of modern strategy is about identifying and better utilizing (or "leveraging") the core competencies of an organization—what it does particularly well. Yet success in the future is most likely to be from the acquisition of new competencies rather than the exploitation of existing ones. Strategy is therefore about what competencies to acquire, and how to acquire them. For example, the traditional organization is:

- self-contained
- hierarchical
- centralized

In contrast, the organization of the future is likely to follow a different model:

- alliance-enabled
- networked
- driven by distributed decision-making (a particular form of decentralization)

The organization that is flexible and innovative enough to master rapidly changing markets will differ markedly from the traditional organization. Management in the old economy is, and has been, directive and controlling. Leadership is more important in the new economy, and it will need to be empowering and coordinating.

Achieving Customer-Centeredness

In a competitive world with such rapid change, attracting and retaining customers and clients becomes crucial. Therefore much discussion centers on organizations becoming more customer-centered. Many leaders believe their organizations have become sufficiently customer-centered in recent years, but the harsh reality is that very few organizations are really customer-oriented. Instead, most organizations fall into one of the three categories:

- Operations-centered
- Transactions-centered
- Technology-centered

It is easy to understand why. In many organizations the largest single group of people is associated with the operations that the organization performs. It becomes relatively simple to convince oneself that the quality and cost-effectiveness of operations are the most important thing to customers. The focus of the organization is on what it does most (operations).

Many companies focus on sales—on transactions with the customers. They mistakenly believe that this is being customer-centered, but in fact, firms that focus heavily on transactions are perfectly capable of almost ignoring true customers' needs and wants. Instead, they are focused on how to get the customer to buy the products or services already being produced by the firm.

Finally, many organizations become enamored of technology. Again, it is quite easy to persuade oneself that what the customer wants and needs is really the fanciest new gadget, or to whatever product he or she buys produced by the most modern technology. These things may matter greatly to the technologists and their hangers-on in the organization, but matter, we know from marketing studies, only to a small portion of customers, who are labeled "early adapters." Far from focusing on the consumer as they mistakenly believe, technology-focused companies often pay attention to only a tiny fraction of their customers—the early adapters.

It is the task of the leader to break through these old patterns of focus in her organization and to replace them with a serious focus on the customer. Only if this is done can a leader begin to feel comfortable that his organization is likely to adapt quickly enough to changes in customer demands.

Setting a Moral Tone

As our economy grows larger and more complex, the opportunities and potential rewards for dishonest behavior grow even more rapidly. Corporate fraud can balloon into the billions. In the case of WorldCom—once one of America's largest and fast-growing companies—bankruptcy following years of fraudulent financial reporting cost investors some $11 billion. During the years of the fraud, top executives of the company had in one way or another taken out about $2 billion.

To avoid such scandals, a key responsibility of the leader is to set a moral tone for her organization. Without a proper moral tone, rules will be ignored, assets stolen, reports falsified, and the organization itself may be imperiled. In recent years many major companies have fallen victim to the lack of a proper moral tone, including Adelphia, Enron, WorldCom, and Citigroup—some of which collapsed and disappeared, others of which have survived.

It is not difficult to point to the need for a proper moral tone in a company, but, unfortunately it can be very difficult for a leader to accomplish. At the core of the matter is a leader's willingness to accept inconvenience, or even financial losses, as the price of maintaining high ethical standards. In order to make clear how a moral tone is set, we turn to a real-life, albeit disguised, example.

Moral Leadership in Practice

John was new to his job. He'd been with the company for seven years as a department manager and had just been promoted to run a division. He moved into his new office, that of a vice president, realizing that he would now have responsibility for not just a hundred people but for several thousand. When he'd been invited to the office of the CEO of the company and told about his promotion, the CEO had said to him, "This is an opportunity for you to demonstrate to us the leadership skills we think you have."

He'd been in his job only a few weeks; he was still learning the ropes; but now he was facing his first real leadership challenge. At least, that's how he saw it. He knew that many people wouldn't see it that way at all. To them this would be a simple matter; he knew that they would even justify what was to him a terrible resolution of the matter on moral grounds! But his view was different.

He saw the situation facing him as a fundamental challenge, one in which his decision would set the moral tone of his organization. If he handled this as a routine matter, he thought, he would never again have an opportunity to make clear to the thousands of people in his division something that was of great importance to him.

Leadership in the Midst of External Change

John signaled his secretary to send in his next appointment. In came a well-dressed, polished executive who headed the largest department in his division. John had known the man for years; they had been peers and friendly rivals when both were department heads, though the other man had managed the larger and more significant department. But John's visitor had been passed over for promotion, and he now came in to meet privately with the peer who had become his boss.

A Difficult Conversation

After rising to greet his visitor, John sat facing him in the seating area in a corner of his office. John made a habit of never facing a person across his desk—it was too formal, reeking too much of authority and impatience. Instead, John always took his visitors to the seating area, where they sat on couch and chair and faced him across a low coffee table.

His visitor smiled wanly. "I shouldn't have done this," he said, opening the conversation.

"No," John agreed, "you shouldn't have."

"I haven't done it before."

"It's clearly out of bounds."

"I know, but it's not much money."

"That doesn't matter."

"I had a great year last year."

"I do not disagree with that. Your department is our division's top producer," John said. "You made the company a lot of money."

His visitor smiled, convinced that he was gaining an advantage.

"Look, I promise I won't do this again."

"I can't let this go," John explained, his expression very serious.

Suddenly a frown slid across his visitor's face. He realized that the conversation wasn't going well at all.

"What do you mean?" he asked.

"There's no second chance on this," John said. "Everyone knows that people can't falsify expense accounts. No rule could be clearer."

His visitor sat without any expression on his face.

"The rules are clear that it's an automatic dismissal if someone does this."

"But you can't mean that," the visitor objected. "I did it only once; it's not much money; and I won't do it again. Besides, I've already returned the money to the company. Isn't that enough?"

John looked at him impassively and said nothing.

The man's face was suddenly ashen. "Look, he said, "you're a religious man. It's supposed to be a good thing to forgive someone."

John hesitated. It was very tempting to let the matter pass. It was going to be damaging to let his top-producing executive go; he'd have to work hard to find a successor. What would

Leadership in the Midst of External Change

the CEO say when he discovered that John had fired his top lieutenant after only a few weeks on the job? Further, the man was obviously very embarrassed and remorseful.

But the rules were there for a reason; and the man looked sorry today, but tomorrow he might decide he could get away with it, or something else, and try it again. If a person could steal from the corporation and John let him remain in a leadership role, what kind of signal did that send to other people? John knew the answer —the wrong kind of signal. John steeled himself to do what he was convinced was right.

"I do forgive you," John said. "Of course I forgive you, though it is not me that you offended, it is the company. But the rules are rules. Forgiveness doesn't mean that there will be no consequences for violating the rules. You have to leave the company. Leave quietly. Understand that I don't want to make a big production of this. I'm not trying to make a public example of you. I know you're a great manager and a hard worker; and I do think you won't ever do something like this again. I'm very happy to help you find a job at another company. But I can't let you stay here."

In the days immediately following, the manager who had falsified his expense account submitted his resignation to John, cleaned out his office, and moved out. John began the process of searching for his replacement.

Just after the man had vacated his office, John was stopped in the hall by a senior employee in his division. There were several other employees standing nearby who were listening. "I just wanted to tell you," the employee began, "that we all know what you did, and we think you were exactly right and we appreciate your doing it."

He smiled at John, shook his hand, and turned away. John noticed that the other employees in the hall were nodding their heads in agreement and some even softly clapped their hands. There had been no need to spell out to what the reference was—it was to the executive John had just dismissed.

In the following days similar compliments for John came from other employees. He realized that what he had thought was a private matter between the offending executive and himself had in fact been a very public occasion—that almost everyone in his division knew about the whole incident—what had caused it, the executive's plea that the matter be dropped, and John's insistence that he must go.

John took his secretary aside and asked her about the matter.

"People know all about this," she said. "They knew the guy was falsifying his expense account, and they knew that it had been reported to you. We all thought…" she continued, then stopped, grinned and corrected herself, "the others thought that you would just let it pass. After all, he's a big executive and a top producer. But you didn't let him get away with it. That sends a huge signal to everyone in the organization that you play it straight."

John hadn't meant to send a signal; he'd only been doing what he thought was right; but he realized that in dismissing the executive he had set exactly the tone that he wanted for his organization—that people obeyed the rules about honesty. He also realized how perilously close he might have come to undermining honesty in his organization had he allowed the man to remain. It had been a big test of his leadership, exactly what the CEO had meant when he gave John the job and told him that it was a chance for John to demonstrate his leadership ability—but it had come at a time and in a form that had almost caused John to miss its significance.

"That's what real leadership is about," John told himself. "It is how we act when we think others aren't watching."

It was only a short time before the man John had fired found a position at another company. When they ran into each other, they were courteous. The man showed no apparent rancor—he seemed to accept that John had done the right thing.

The CEO seemed to agree. Eight years later when the CEO retired, John moved into the top position in the company.

Moral Leadership When Attitudes Are Shifting

Social mores are changing continually. Behavior which was not accepted yesterday is tolerated today and may become common tomorrow. There are strong differences between generations in what is socially accepted and what is not. Organizations must make choices in this environment of ethical change and uncertainty.

It is often argued that an important quality of leadership is to demonstrate moral courage and ethical behavior—to set an example of both for a leader's organization. But it is difficult for a leader to set an example that all or even most will accept and that doesn't threaten to polarize opinion rather than to create commonality. How does a leader respond to these very significant challenges?

This is another topic too often discussed in generalities. It is easy to refer to broad principles in a way that satisfies every reader, so that the reality of the difficult choices involved is obscured. People studying leadership think they've learned something about moral leadership, but often the general propositions are of no use in application. It is said, for example, that a leader must stand by his principles. No one disagrees. But a deeper understanding begins only when we address what that means in a specific context. To address this vital issue, we will examine in detail the true story (though we will not reveal the company's name) of a young CEO and a major ethical dilemma.

A young software engineer finished business school and immediately started his own company. He was its CEO. For the first two years he worked hard to raise money to support the company, to assemble a good team of programmers, and to design and begin to build the software that was to be the center of his company's product offering. Broadly speaking, his company was designing new software for companies that used the Internet extensively.

After two years of development, the company was ready to take its first products to market. He began to hire a sales team. He raised more money, but the ongoing operating costs of the organization had begun to outstrip what money he could raise from investors, and so he had to bring in revenues from clients. Soon customer accounts began to trickle in.

In the fourth year the company had a growing staff of product developers, a number of salespersons, and a few good customer accounts. The top executive team, now grown to several people, established an aggressive business plan. Sales were supposed to grow by eighty percent in the upcoming year. The start was slow, but in the fourth month of the year a salesperson brought in a large potential account—one that would account for almost half of the sales target for the entire year. That one client could mean that the company would fulfill its sales target for the year and that his attention and that

Leadership in the Midst of External Change

of his management team could be turned to the next milestone in the company's development.

There was, however, one problem. The potential customer who could do so much good for the company was not just an ordinary firm—it was a major online pornography company. The salesperson disclosed this to the CEO with a wry smile, recognizing that a decision had to be made—to accept the business or not.

The CEO realized instantly that this might be a moment of definition in his leadership of the company. He could accept the business and it would signal that his firm was business-oriented first and foremost; he could refuse it and signal that ethical standards mattered as well as business opportunities. He was CEO; it was his call to make.

But he thought first that he should find out what others in his team thought about the matter. In a few conversations he discovered that several of his top management group didn't object at all to doing business with a pornography company; but there were others who objected vigorously—so vigorously, that they suggested that if the company accepted business of that nature, they might leave.

The matter was fast becoming a testing-case of the CEO's ethical standards. He couldn't delay long—the salesperson was anxious to get back to the pornography company with an acceptance of their order; he was concerned that they'd take their business to a competitor. He consulted privately again with his top management team, and selected people from the programming, sales and administrative staff who were opinion leaders and sought their reactions to the issue. Soon everyone in the company knew that the question was on the CEO's desk.

His decision was complicated by the fact that his company was still perfecting its products, so that a customer didn't simply buy something off the shelf, but worked quite closely with his company to develop the capabilities of the product. A client company became not just an arms-length customer but almost a partner of his firm in product development. The question was, therefore, should he permit his company to partner with a pornography company?

Opinions in the company began to polarize. Some of his associates couldn't understand his hesitation. Pornography is a big part of online business activity, how could his company stay out of it, they asked? The company needed sales, and here was a huge potential order; he should immediately accept it, they said. To reject the customer on the grounds of morality was overly conservative, they insisted, when there was a big market for pornography and when doing business with such a company wasn't illegal. The CEO's responsibility, they said, was to place the interests of the company before any of his own preconceived attitudes toward morality. Consequently, it is neither acceptable nor ethical, they claimed, for him to place his or other individual's personal moral views above the interests of the company, its employees and investors. Attitudes toward what is moral, and what is not, vary from person to person in our country, they said, and a company cannot base its choice of customers on such shifting opinions.

The opponents of the sale were equally insistent. To them pornography was a moral evil—something that in some of its forms remained illegal in many countries. Should the company accept the customer, then a significant part of its business would become facilitating the online distribution of pornography. The company would be indirectly in the pornography business! It would derive a significant portion of its income from pornography. From being proud to be working with a company that was trying to improve the flow of information and commerce in the world, they would in effect have suddenly become little more than second-hand pornographers. How could they face their families and friends if this were the case? By accepting the business the CEO would be, therefore, placing each of them in a very uncomfortable ethical position.

The CEO recognized that he needed to handle the situation carefully—that if he took any of a set of possible actions, he could stumble badly. For example, it was very tempting to make the decision boldly as an expression of his own ethical standards, trying to set a tone for his entire organization. Wasn't this what leadership demanded, he asked himself?

But he realized that in the highly charged atmosphere of his company, in which people differed so much in their opinions about what was right and wrong, the reaction to any decision of his (for or against taking the new business) was going to be predictable. Those who supported his decision would welcome it; the others would think that he had badly overreached by imposing his personal moral views on the company. They would think of it as a kind of ego-trip: "He thinks it's his company and he can do with it whatever he wants," they would say. This was not a message he wanted to send, since he was trying to create a corporate culture in which everyone thought of himself or herself as a participating owner (if only psychologically) of the firm.

So he decided that it would be an error to conceive the requirement of leadership to require that he should make a decision about morality for the company himself. Nor did he want to spend time and effort researching the morality of pornography in its various forms, then make a decision and try to justify it via education and persuasion to his employees. This was going beyond his competence, he thought.

But he'd noticed in his discussions with others in his organization that, by and large the people who opposed taking the pornographers' business felt much more strongly about it than those who supported it. Also, other salespersons were bringing in business steadily—at a pace that might well attain the sales targets set for the year (though not so quickly and so profitably as would accepting the pornography contract).

The CEO's Decision

So in the end the young CEO declined the business. He told his top managers, and each explained to the people in his or her department, that he thought it was not his role as CEO to make a moral choice for the company, but that he had based his decision on what he had learned from talking to his staff. Those who opposed taking the business were stronger in their opinions—they worried that it would undermine respect for them personally at home, and in the community—than those who supported taking the business. In addition, he noted, the company was likely to meet its sales targets anyway.

He explained that he could have put the matter to a formal vote among the top management team of the company, but he'd already learned from his private discussions how each member of the team felt about the issue, and it was his job as CEO, he thought, to make the final decision for the firm.

There was some grumbling from the sales staff and the top managers who had wanted the business, but that was all. The CEO received heart-felt thanks from those who had opposed the business.

Leadership in the Midst of External Change

Two years later the company was much larger; it had many new managers. The issue came up again, but the contract was of much less importance to the company financially. Now the company's products were at a more advanced stage of development, and new customers didn't actually partner with the company. So the pornography company would be merely one of many arms-length purchasers of the company's products. This time there was virtually no opposition to the sale, and the company accepted the business.

How to Avoid a Company That Won't Change

When business leaders publicly comment on the "inertia of people not wanting to change" at their companies, it can be frightening to think that any of us could join an organization that is unwilling to change. It can be a personal disaster to land in such an organization because in a world that changes rapidly and requires adaptation, companies that are rigid often disappear, and with them the careers of people who worked hard for them.

Yet the danger is real, because many corporations are quite fixed in their ways and a person can find herself squeezed in between a supervisor and level of subordinates who are unwilling to try something different. If a company is not committed to change, -it will be next to impossible to have a successful career within its ranks, because it is not likely to survive long enough.

We might think: "I'm a victim of an organization that is unwilling to change." It's not only frustrating, but has the potential of being destructive to our hopes and plans. How long should we stick it out to try and make a difference by helping lead the company toward necessary change? When, if at all, should we call it quits and move on? All of these concerns address the challenge of trying to do great things in an environment that normally just won't allow it.

When we're busy interviewing companies to see about a job, we can protect ourselves from being sucked into organizations that won't change by the type of questions we ask. Therefore it becomes important to talk to the leaders of an organization to try to figure out where they've been, what they've done, and how their careers have changed over the past 10 to 15 years—and how they've responded and dealt with the changes. Also, it is important to ask about how the company deals with employees who want to switch functions—for example, are your supervisors likely to support your move within the company or will they oppose it because you're valuable to their department?

Lisa gives us an example from her personal experience:

> "I was very fortunate in my last job to work for a company where change was the rule, rather than the exception. Most of the supervisors and managing directors in my group had worked in different geographies, in different functions, in completely different roles—yet each of them valued this experience as a chance for growth and as important in defining how they currently led others."

Another often-useful approach when thinking about a job offer is to talk to the junior people in the firm. Unfortunately many senior people tell an applicant exactly what she wants to hear—they are often trying to sell the applicant on the job and the company. Ask to spend a day in the office and get people to one side and ask them for their honest opinion—it usually comes out and is very useful.

Companies Facing Change

For those companies who do face significant external change, there are specific actions we can take to effectively handle the situation.

Leadership in the Midst of External Change

There are six steps that a leader can take in this scenario:

- Create a vision of the organization and its success in the future
- Build a culture suitable to the new setting
- Develop people for the new setting
- Clear the decks of unwanted politics
- Demonstrate your high personal character
- Reinvent yourself as a leader when necessary

The vision needs to be clear and inspiring. Building the new culture must be done explicitly; we must know what we are doing. Don't let mores simply emerge. Plan for the desired attitudes and behaviors and lead people to them.

In developing people, don't think of people as interchangeable items; think of each as a unique combination of capabilities and try to get the most out of each, or alternatively to let each develop himself to herself to their potential. People bring valuable ideas – about products and services to make money; and about how to cut costs.

When clearing the decks, be sure the organization is set up so people can succeed; avoid too much politics—when you observe it in the organization, ask yourself, "Am I causing this?" Did I set up an organization that made politics profitable for people in their careers? If the answers to these questions are "Yes," then shift direction. A simple rule is that to change the culture of an organization (from one of lots of non-useful politicking, for example), change the behavior of the leader.

Leadership: How to Lead, How to Live

On the question of personal character, remember that leaders are and should be held to higher standards than others. A person's base for leadership can be of different types, but whatever the base or bases, he or she must earn the moral authority to lead others through humility, accessibility and an appreciation for the contributions of others.

On the question of reinvention, the hardest challenge here may be to recognize when we need to change ourselves.

"I reinvented myself five times as a leader during my career," a former CEO said. "The company was growing fast and my style of leadership was repeatedly made obsolete. I had to learn new skills, and shift my base for leadership."

The signs will be there, but other people may not tell us, or even deny what the signs are saying. This is because some people flatter leaders in an attempt to get favorable treatment, and others don't want to bring bad news, for fear they'll be blamed. Hence the importance of humility and accessibility and appreciation for others each of which contributes to encouraging others to be honest with us.

Queen Elizabeth I of England understood the importance of getting honest feedback and advice from her close associates. When she made William Cecil her prime minister (he lasted for 40 years), she gave him this assignment: "Don't be corrupted by any form of gift; be loyal to England; tell me the truth—your honest views—always."

CHAPTER REFERENCES:

Gardner, John. **On Leadership**. New York: The Free Press, 1990.

ADDITIONAL READINGS:

Redmond, Andrea and Charles A. Tribbett III. **Business Evolves, Leadership Endures.** Westport, Connecticut: Easton Studio Press, Russell Reynolds Associates, 2004.

Leadership: How to Lead, How to Live

PART IV

THE PLACE OF LEADERSHIP IN OUR LIVES

Leadership: How to Lead, How to Live

Chapter 13

Sustaining Leadership Via a Balanced Life

Intellect alone won't lead you to make the right choices—won't, in fact, take you down the right path. You have to master not only the art of listening to your head, you must also master listening to your heart.

- Carly Fiorina, former Hewlett-Packard CEO

Leadership: How to Lead, How to Live

For many of us leadership is a life-long quest. As we climb the career ladder, we have a broader range in which to exercise leadership. But unless we are careful, other things that are also important can get squeezed out of our lives. Why? Because being a leader often requires a very high commitment to professional activities and is possible, therefore, only at the risk of a high cost to our personal lives.

It is also possible, of course, that we become leaders in volunteer work or in an avocation, in which case leadership threatens to exact a high cost in both our careers and family lives. If we give up too much of our personal lives to our careers, or too much of our family life to leadership activities in volunteer work or our hobbies, then there comes a day when we're burnt out—either exhausted or so full of regret for what we've lost that we can't go on.

To avoid such a disastrous result, we need balance in our lives. Being a successful leader in business or in the not-for-profit world doesn't guarantee us success in other aspects of our lives; and it doesn't guarantee us a balanced life; it tends to do the opposite. The more successful we are as leaders, the more claims work places on our time and energy.

In this chapter we will examine the importance of work/life balance in our lives, and means of attaining it.

Finding a balance remains important for two key reasons: it's necessary to keep a person fresh and of good mental health in his or her work; and it is necessary to avoid demoralizing regret at a later stage in life. Finding a balance is challenging, however; so find your personal strategy and stay with it!

The Conflict

We often receive advice to put first things first. We can do this, but a challenge arises when we have more than one first thing. In most of our lives our careers are very important but so are our personal lives. If we put career before the other aspects of our lives, we are likely to get involved in difficult emotional stress that interfere with our success on the job. If we put those other aspects of our lives, including family, before career, we may not succeed in the competitive tussle that is career advancement.

Balance between the two is crucial to our long-term ability to lead others without getting detoured into stress, tension, regrets and even withdrawal. There are a number of factors involved:

- For most people there is an inherent conflict between career needs and the other aspects of their lives.

- The pressures of work are quite intense since most companies expect people to focus on work related issues at the expense of the family. Even if companies say they don't do this, they often behave as if they do.

- Most people who have children when asked to list their priorities put them in this order: spouse and children; career.

- Many people who say that family is first spend most of their waking hours at work.

- Most people who have no children place friends and hobbies at the top of the list of their priorities with career. But often they have little time for anything but work.

Most people want to achieve a balance between career and other aspects of their lives; why is this so rarely done? Are people hypocrites—do they really prefer to work? Or is it difficult to find the right balance?

Kevin's Story

Kevin was an extremely successful executive. He was in his late forties and running the largest division of a major multinational company. One day the CEO of the firm called him into his office and told him that he was next in line to run the firm. He was very excited. He hurried home that evening to tell his wife:

He'd expected her to be as excited as he was. She wasn't. She looked at him steadily during a long pause before she answered, then said, "If you do, then the children and I will be gone."

Kevin was stunned by her reaction. He stifled an impulse to get angry and instead asked, "Why?"

Controlling her own temper, she responded, "You were out of town over two hundred nights last year." She paused again, to let him object if he wanted to. He didn't. Instead, he nodded, indicating that he knew what she said was true.

"If you're CEO," she continued, "won't it be the same?"

Kevin understood where she was going. He had no desire to try to mislead her. "No," he said, "it'll be worse."

She nodded. "I thought so," she said. Then she continued, "You hardly know our children. Susan has written an essay in school about how you're never around. You weren't there, she wrote, when she hurt her knee. You weren't there, she wrote, when she climbed a tree."

Kevin could hardly breathe; he was stunned. None of this had he heard before.

"And Bobby is going into high school this year. Did you go to any of his ball games last year?"

"One," Kevin offered quietly.

His wife smiled wanly. "Yes," she said, "one. I forgot you'd made even one."

For the next several days Kevin wrestled with himself in a way he'd never done before. His wife had told him the truth. He hardly knew his children, and he saw little of her. His wife and children had a different life than his. He was too busy in his career.

If he took the CEO position, he'd see even less of them. In effect, taking the position was abandoning his family. His wife was right to say they'd leave.

He thought about his friends who were also high-level business executives. Many of them were divorced; many had children they hardly knew. Some of them, he knew, were filled with regrets.

After a week had passed, Kevin went to the CEO of his firm and said he couldn't accept the position. He expected that the CEO would be upset. But instead he asked why.

"Because," Kevin answered, "I'll lose my family if I take the job."

The CEO nodded. "I understand," he said. "And I respect your decision. I sometimes think I should have done the same thing."

With his eyes opened to his family's feelings, Kevin didn't remain long in his position as division president. It also took too much of his time. He left the big company, joined a smaller one where he'd have much more time with his family, and never looked back.

Misapprehensions About Work/Life Balance

Many people mislead themselves about work/family balance. Among the most common beliefs are:

- I can work hard early in my career and find time for my family later.

- I can work and my spouse can take care of the children, and such specialization gives us a balance.

- If I'm with my spouse and children, I have balance.

Each of these common beliefs is in fact a misapprehension.

The "Make Time Later" Myth. A person who tries to work hard early in his career in order to find time later for his family often ends up like Kevin—regretting the time he didn't have with his family. The reason is that each stage of our career has its own challenges and rewards.

When we're successful early on, we realize that we can do much more from higher-level positions. Most of us also enjoy what we do well, and since we've been successful at the office, we want to spend even more time and accomplish even more. Our self-images become intertwined with our work.

We're not comfortable except in the work environment. Even when we take time to be with our families, we would often rather be at work. Families are fairly unexciting compared to a career circling the globe for a multi-national company; or even dealing with major disasters for a mission-driven not-for-profit organization.

As we get more responsibility in an organization, we find that more and more people depend on us. When Kevin turned down the CEO job, he was startled to discover than within a few days, many people in his own division knew what he had done. He was even more startled to realize that they were very angry with him. They had tied their own careers to his (he was the "shooting star"), and when he flamed out, they saw their own hopes of advancement set back.

Was his own family so much more important to him, they demanded, than they were? He wanted to say no, that they were both important to him, but as he thought about it, he realized that for years he had acted as if his companions at work were more important to him than his family; and now he was acting as if his family was more important to him than his companions at work. "Why couldn't I," Kevin asked himself, "have behaved as if both were important to me all along?"

The Division of Labor Myth. When a couple tries to take care of their children by having one work continually and the other stay home, this does not really provide a balance in their lives. The parent who is at work loses touch with the rest of the family. And he or she doesn't get to enjoy other important elements of life than work alone. The other parent would probably love to get out of the house more; to have a career on his or her own. Having both parents with unbalanced lives doesn't create a balance for the pair.

The "Quality Time" Myth. For many successful people who take time to be with their families, the time isn't really spent with them at all. Instead it's spent on the phone to work, or doing email for work, or thinking about work. The body is there, but not the mind and not the spirit.

Strategies to Achieve Balance

People try to follow one of three different strategies for balance. Some do so knowingly; others don't realize clearly what they are doing (just as for many years Kevin didn't). They are not objective about themselves. The three strategies are:

- Balancing week by week.
- Balancing over a year.
- Balancing via a short career.

Balancing Week by Week

Those of us who follow this strategy are not comfortable postponing balance; instead, we want to try to achieve it throughout our lives. In effect, we set a goal that there should never a significant imbalance. We allocate a significant amount of time every week—every day if we can—to our non-work priorities.

This can be very hard to achieve for a person who is climbing a career ladder and exercising more and more leadership at work. But it is sometimes possible if we find a position in a company in which work demands are not too great. Doing so all but rules out a career in many industries—including investment banking and consulting, for example, or in entrepreneurial efforts. Careers in these areas generally involve too much travel and too long hours for a person to have balance in their lives on a continuous basis.

Carole was at the top of her class at college. When she graduated, she had many employment offers. Some brought substantial salaries, but also demanded very long hours of work and lots of travel. While those offers were exciting, she wasn't willing to give up other aspects of her life. So she looked for a company where she could work hard but also have some time free from work. Her target was to spend some time each day with her friends and family. She was prepared to give up some salary and some rapidity of career advance for those things.

Balancing Over a Year

This is a common strategy. Its key notion is that while I have to work very long hours during the week, I can spend my weekends doing other things. Or that, while I have to work very hard during this particular season (like retail managers during the holiday season), I will have time during the rest of the year, including my vacation, for other things. In general:

- There is no balance at any single point in time, but when a person looks back there is an overall balance during the year.

- The idea is to work to the exclusion of other things some of the year, and then do other things to the exclusion of work at other times during the year.

Sylvia is the CEO of a moderately sized business in which there are 3,000 employees. There are many days she must spend long hours at the office, but there are also some times when she can get away early to coach her children's soccer teams. Those times are not only pleasing to her children, but they are valuable to her because they get her out of the office and freshen her thinking. Although she almost never achieves a balance between work and other things during a single day, over the course of a year she achieves a bit of balance.

Balancing Via a Short Career

Many of us are ambitious people who are seeking to attain positions of leadership in organizations and who believe that if we work very long hours in the early years of our careers, we can climb reasonably quickly to a position in which we control our own schedules and can then allocate much more time to our non-work lives. Thus, we plan to have a short career, and we have a target date for switching from "all work" to a more balanced life.

Some of us formulate our strategy a bit differently. We believe that we can work very hard for fifteen years or so and become relatively financially secure. Then we can retire early, have a family, and devote ourselves to it. This "get rich quick" strategy can work. A number of people have pulled it off in recent years, especially during the dot.com boom of the late 1990s.

Sometimes those of us who pursue a short-career strategy postpone having a family until our target date for a switch in the orientation of our lives. Sometimes we start a family well before the target date, but we won't pay much attention to our spouse and children until the target date arrives.

Barney obtained his computer engineering degree at a major university. Then we went to work for two high tech start-ups. He spent two years at one; then two years at the other. Then he went to business school.

From his first day at business school he was thinking about how to start his own company when he graduated. He gathered some friends and found a bit of money from a backer and started the company a month after getting his MBA. He put all his life into his business. He worked long hours and seven days a week. His friends were in the business. He had a string of girlfriends but lost each one as she would realize that he wasn't going to commit to a stable relationship until his business was fully established. His plan was to spend fifteen years building the business, then sell it and retire. He'd be forty-two at the time he retired. Then he'd have leisure to marry and have a family, and he'd have time to spend with them.

When asked about his life outside the company, he'd respond that he didn't have one. At the time of this writing Barney's company is five years old. There's no way at this point to know if his strategy will succeed or fail.

Barney's is a very attractive strategy to many people, but its success is very uncertain. Never have more than a few people managed to get rich early in their careers; and the number has been declining as the economy has been less expansive than in the past.

The fundamental flaw in the strategy is that most of us will either:

- Not attain the desired level in our careers—at which we shift our priorities from work to family—as quickly as we hoped, so we go right past our target date and the turning point drags on and on, with our focus remaining on business.

- Or, get so involved in our careers that when the target date comes, we don't want to make the shift that we've planned in our priorities. Work has become fun, it's all consuming, and we just don't want to put it aside.

There's yet another risk for the strategy of a short career, and that is that if we have a family early on, and don't devote time to spouse and children, then even if our strategy succeeds, and we achieve our target date, then when we decide to leave work and focus on our families, our spouse may have other interests and our children may be largely grown up. We suddenly have time for them, but they've created lives that don't include us, and we end up with career success and an empty life regretting what we've missed.

Ways to Maintain Work/Life Balance

There are careers that do not lend themselves to work/life balance; they take too much time and concentration—there's no room for anything else. We kid ourselves if we take a job like this, and say we're also going to have a balanced life.

So we have to decide what's important to us, and if work isn't the major thing, then we have to consciously decide to attain balance by:

- Picking a career and a job that permits us to have time for non-work commitments, and;

- Leaving a career, if we're already in it, that takes so much time that we have no opportunity for balance.

But even if we carefully select a career that offers time enough for balance, we can still let ourselves get too much involved in work. To avoid this trap, therefore, we should:

- Treat an appointment or outing with family or friends exactly like a meeting with a top executive in your organization Give it that kind of high priority.

- Try not to take work problems home. For example, use the entire commute home to get into a family frame of mind. Be present mentally and emotionally when you're at home or with your friends.

- Tell the most pressing business problem you can think of to a young child—it will remind you how ridiculous some of these problems seem and make it easier to leave them at work.

One of the keys to finding balance is understanding ourselves and seeing clearly how we are behaving. Here, friends and family can help in giving us an "outside" view of our progress towards balance.

The Family-Friendly Corporation

The previous strategies have all focused on personal strategies to achieve work-life balance. But some companies have encouraged an environment that supports rather than penalizes people for leaving the office to attend family sporting and social events. Some companies create an atmosphere that is family-friendly by:

- Encouraging employees to attend family sporting and social events.

- Sponsoring family events.

- Understanding that, though the needs and goals of the company are never to be sacrificed, each individual's family is important!

Karen worked for a small consulting firm that has made true work-life balance a part of its culture, in stark contrast to many major consulting firms at which balance exists, for the most part, in theory only. The top managers at Karen's firm have entrenched this balance in their culture primarily through their own examples. Everyone, including the CEO, leaves the office by 7 PM every evening.

If Karen was wrapped up in what she was doing and tried to stay later, her manager would practically force her out the door. The vice president who had hired her had proposed an arrangement with the firm before he accepted his own employment offer in order to maintain the balance in his life. At the time, his children were in school, so he placed a cap on the number of days per year he would travel. He also convinced the company to allow (and pay for) his wife to travel with him whenever she so desired. This arrangement was important because the work/life balance was then such that he would be able to spend quality time on the road with her after he returned from working with clients. Because of the culture promoted by the CEO, the firm agreed to these conditions. To this day, despite the fact that the vice president is extremely passionate about his job and has enormous responsibility—he's second in the chain of command—he has a wonderful relationship with his wife and children as well as numerous hobbies.

Leaders who promote work/life balance by living it themselves can successfully embed it as part of the culture of their organizations so that it becomes real for others. The firm Karen works for is extremely successful, and is recognized as a worldwide leader in its segment of industry. Its employees appear to be happy and productive.

Karen found she had made some trade offs in working for this firm. Her compensation was 15 percent less than she could have obtained at a firm with a "work-all-the-time" culture.

The firm is not as well known as others, so that her resume isn't as impressive as it would be if she had chosen to work for a better-known firm. But she had found a challenging and rewarding working environment that also permitted significant work/life balance.

The currency of business is money; the currency of relationships is time. Don't get them mixed up!

Money makes business go; it's how we pay for resources and how people show that they value what we provide (that is, by being our customers and paying us for what they buy).

Time makes relationships strong; it's a key method by which people show that they care about each other.

If we should try, as many people do, to mix the two, the result can be disastrous. Many people have great difficulty in their personal and professional lives because they try to substitute money for time as the currency of their relationships.

People who put their careers first in life often assert that they are doing it in order to provide a higher income and better life for their families; and sometimes this is true. But often for high achievers in our wealthy economy, there is something different going on.

A person who is working all the time because he or she wants to is often doing so because he wants to excel; it's a bit of an ego-trip. So he justifies his behavior as necessary to support his family. This means that he ends up trying to base his family relationships on the currency of business (money); he's not basing his relationships on their proper currency—time. He's too busy at work to spend time with his family.

Too often a person doing this doesn't ask if that's what his family wants—they might say no; that they want more of his time—and he doesn't want to hear that. So he continues to work too much and justify it as necessary to provide a comfortable high-level life style for his family.

Similarly, people sometimes try to substitute in business the currency of relationships. A salesman in a firm might have a target for sales, and when she fails to meet it, she relies on her friendship with her manager to try to keep her job. When her manager says, "You didn't make your quota; this isn't the job for you. You'd be better doing something else," she responds, "You're being mean to me; I thought we were friends. How can you treat a friend this way?"

There is room for friendship in business, but not as a substitute for the financial performance expected of people.

Given the amount of time most of us spend at work, it's only natural to develop some relationships that extend beyond the workplace. Difficult situations can arise that test our ability to maintain a balance between the two dimensions—friendship and economics—of a business relationship. A business exists for the purpose of financial success. It's a business, after all, not a club. So its primary currency is money. Financial success is what it's about first and foremost.

Douglas helped start a company with four other colleagues who had known each other for some five years outside of work. All came from similar backgrounds (investment banking), but had never worked directly with one another. Being thrown into an intense working environment definitely changed their relationships; Doug realized that his friendships would never again be the same. For him it was a bitter pill to swallow.

But when he realized that at work business had to come first, and friendship second, and adapted to this, then he was able to be grateful to be working with friends. There was a level of trust and loyalty among the group of friends that didn't disappear because they were now in a business environment, and carried with it high morale to the workplace.

When we offer money in lieu of time to those who love us; and offer time and affection in lieu of financial performance to those we work for; then we are trying to pay debts in the wrong currency, and such a reversal often fails.

The Importance of Giving Attention to Work/Life Balance Early

It is important for each of us to think seriously about the issue of work/life balance early in our careers. What balance we may desire will differ a great between us; but by focusing on the matter early on, we are likely to avoid serious errors. It is important for us to reflect on what makes us happy, so that we avoid making wrong choices that we then have to get out of, perhaps damaging our careers and filling our lives with regrets—including unnecessarily scarring our own lives and others who are close to us.

The best way for each of us to determine the optimal balance for our own lives may very well be trial and error. We should engage in a process of continual trial and error—supporting reflection throughout our careers—rather than blindly charging ahead toward a goal, as so many people do for most of their careers.

Regina was asked how she found time for both a dramatic career and her family. "If I had aimed all my energy at my daughter," Regina responded, "I'd have driven her crazy."

Regina's comment reminds us that there is time for both career and family for most of us. But when we're young and before we have a family, it may seem that the sky is the limit when pursuing our goals. Then we when acquire a family, a spouse's interests and goals, the needs of children, and similar considerations have to be taken into account—in fact, our careers are no longer simply our own; our families have a vested interest in what we do; and we should include them in the decision-making process.

Ambition comes in many forms, and at its extreme, can be blind. We want to be able to avoid blindness, to see the impact of our career decisions on others and ultimately on ourselves, and to do this in advance of bad decisions, not simply afterwards in reflection.

The Role of Friendships in Work/Life Balance

When we're leaving college many of us do not yet have spouses and children, and our primary relationships are with friends. But when we have our own families, and are pursuing a career, then often we sacrifice our friends to find enough time for work and family. Can those of us with careers and families make time to spend in friendships, or must friends become a second priority?

For many of us having good friends is really important and helps to keep us grounded and in tune with other people and their perspectives. Friends can help us through work and personal issues, and so can be invaluable.

Yet as our lives progress, with the pressure of career and family, and with our meeting new people all the time, friendships tend, by necessity, to become based more on convenience (for example, being friends with someone on your child's sports team) than on a true bond, based on shared values, dreams, and spirits.

The most fortunate of us will continue to make an effort to retain old friends and add new, realizing how important they are to us.

Can Successful Careers Coexist with Normal Family Life?

This is an issue with which many people struggle daily.

It should be discussed at length—how does a couple balance one partner's career against the other's? What do we do if one person has a great opportunity in one city and the other person in another city? If we have children, whose responsibility are they? There may not be a once-and-for-all solution. Instead, we may have to apply our priorities on a case-by-case basis and continually reevaluate our priorities themselves.

Certainly two careers do coexist with a happy family life for many people. Perhaps the parents don't get to coach a little league team, or go to every soccer game, but they make it to dinner every night and still have time to go over their kid's homework. But there are certainly situations in which a couple cannot both be high profile, career-focused individuals while also being meaningful parents.

If a couple wants a family, then it may be necessary for one parent to eschew as demanding a career as he or she might otherwise pursue. Effective parenting requires much time, love and commitment, so that if two people are so career-focused that neither is willing to sacrifice at least some of his or her career for parenting—then should they chose to be parents in the first place?

Many couples have made their way through these questions in recent years. In most cases it appears that the woman in the couple decided to take time off and slow her career progression down for a while when she had children. But many of these women returned to work after a while (varying from two months to several years) and still had the opportunity to have significant professional achievements in their careers.

If this occurs, it is important that one or the other partner not impose the decision but instead that it is believed by both people to be the best alternative for the couple. Otherwise, blaming and resentment in the future can be strongly unhealthy for the relationship.

When a very successful woman executive was asked how her husband dealt with her success, she responded, "It helped that he also had a successful career."

They had worked out the difficult issues that often face two-career families, including finding single geographical locations where both members of a couple can find great career opportunities. Unfortunately, often one member of a couple feels that he or she is sacrificing the quality of his or her career in order for both to find jobs in the same city. Since this often happens, a most important thing is that both partners are upfront with one another about career aspirations, willingness to travel, desire to have one parent at home with the children, etc. It is far better to even over-communicate than to let any feelings of resentment build up.

Conclusion

Family and work are the two most important priorities in the lives of many of us, but we seemingly don't know how to reconcile them, and this causes tremendous stress and frustration. Discovering a method of reconciling the two would contribute to our peace of mind.

Sustaining Leadership Via a Balanced Life

Balance is very important to us all. Yvette had a consulting assignment one year. She was teaching maintenance managers to use more preventive and predictive techniques as part of their overall equipment maintenance strategy. One fact she often quoted was that it costs three times more to maintain a piece of equipment if it is simply run until it breaks down, rather than being cared for over time using routine maintenance and changing parts based on equipment history. This ratio of three to one in excessive costs is likely to be even more skewed in our personal lives if we neglect our health and relationships.

Leadership: How to Lead, How to Live

CHAPTER REFERENCES:

Mills, D. Quinn. **Having It All....and Making It Work: Six Steps for Putting Both Your Career and Your Family First**. New York: Prentice Hall, 2004.

Leadership: How to Lead, How to Live

Chapter 14

Leadership and Personal Fulfillment

We make a living by what we get, we make a life by what we give.

- Winston Churchill, British prime minister

Leadership: How to Lead, How to Live

Leadership is an important component of our lives; it is not, however, the only thing in our lives, nor for many of us, the most important thing. Each of us must define and pursue his or her own path to personal fulfillment. This chapter is concerned with the broader context of leadership in a person's life.

Does a person who has leadership potential have an obligation to others to use it, or can he or she choose instead to have a quiet life? This question raises another. What is success in life, and how does leadership fit into it? Our goal is that people who exercise leadership should be able to do so effectively throughout their lives, and that leadership fits so well into their lives that disappointments elsewhere do not cause them to abandon being leaders.

A Responsibility to Lead?

Many of us have not only the capacity and ability to lead, but also derive a significant sense of intrinsic reward from the impact we can have on others through our leadership. Yet not all of us make the career and family choices needed to exercise leadership of steadily increasing scope. Do we have a responsibility to do so—an obligation to lead? If we say yes to that question, do we keep the same answer if exercising leadership interferes with our relationships with our family and friends?

On the one hand, sometimes we are best suited for leadership, and if we don't do it, the mission of our organizations will suffer. Those with great leadership potential who would keep it from the world are holding back gifts that would enrich many, but to accept the hardships and sacrifices of leadership must be a choice. Similarly, anyone who enters a leadership position only because he or she feels it is a responsibility may not have the heart to stick through it when "the going gets tough."

Sometimes leadership involves sacrifices that others won't make, and if we don't make them, then again an important mission will suffer. Is it selfish not to accept the mantle of leadership in these situations?

If our gifts for leadership are great, and if we are graced with opportunities to lead on a large scale, we should think broadly about how we can have the greatest impact. Perhaps, then, the matter should not be a matter of amassing the greatest wealth, fame, or power, but rather a profound sense of responsibility to act upon those gifts and push ourselves to fulfill our potential.

Leadership: How to Lead, How to Live

Those who are endowed with the capacity to lead may believe themselves responsible to serve others on one level or another. Many may also find that serving others is a key to happiness. A leader impacts others best when he or she is sincere in desire to serve them; when he or she is passionate about the arena that he is hoping to influence. Those who see leadership as a gift for service to others, feel that they should act upon it.

There is, however, a different point of view. Recognizing that it is our choice what we do with our leadership skills, this view rejects the notion that we have a responsibility to lead people; or to affect the world in one way or another.

It is our right to choose what to do with our lives, this argument insists. Should a person gifted with leadership skills choose instead to join a dance troupe, or to work in a secluded bookstore in a rural area, he or she should be free to do so without a feeling of guilt or of failing to meet expectations of others. Put at its most direct, this point of view is that we do not owe others our leadership skills.

What Defines Personal Fulfillment?

Leadership can be many things, but it always involves a very high commitment of attention and time. To some people it is primarily an opportunity to serve others. To other people it is primarily a route to success. So in determining where leadership fits into our lives, we need to consider the many conceptions people have of what constitutes personal fulfillment. What, we ask, is most important in a person's life?

Leadership and Life

Family: For a great many of us, fulfillment in life is sought in relationships with our families. The satisfaction of having a loving relationship, of raising children, of time spent with relatives—these are the key elements in our lives.

Career Accomplishment: Others of us may focus on what we've accomplished in our careers, often as leaders. We see the meaning of life in pride in what we've accomplished; in our impact on the world. We may ask: who turns to me for advice; who is interested in my views: have I made an important contribution to others? If so, then my life is successful and I'm fulfilled by it.

Widening Opportunities: Other of us see life less as a goal-directed enterprise than as a journey that continues throughout our lives. What is important to us is that the journey steadily opens wider horizons for ourselves (for example, higher positions in business, perhaps chances for government service). In this view, successful people must make difficult and conflicted decisions that are best made by prioritizing the opportunities we face. Our goal is to broaden our choice of opportunities. This is why many of us go to college and some on to advanced degrees—to widen the opportunities we have in life.

A Life Balanced Between Career and Family: Many of us seek a balanced life, what we might call a "full" life, focused on career and family. In the previous chapter we discussed balance as necessary to preserving our leadership for the long term in our lives—but here it becomes an objective in itself. Balance is thought the key to personal fulfillment in life. Those of us who take this view are willing to sacrifice some career advancement for a good home life, and vice versa. The notion is akin to the golden mean advocated by ancient Greek philosophers—that everything should be in moderation.

Comfort: Some of us are satisfied to be comfortable, to enjoy life; often this doesn't mean extravagant living, but instead a moderate lifestyle. We want to have enough money to show our children the world—to visit our family members wherever they may be living—and to be able to splurge on professional sports and nice dinners.

Satisfaction and Lack of Regrets: Others of us look with satisfaction on decisions we've made as central to our conception of life. We wish to avoid regrets of the type we've seen people express in this book. We want to look forward to each tomorrow as bringing as much joy as we experienced yesterday. We want our friends and family close by. We lead because of a desire to do so—and find satisfaction in helping others to succeed on their life journeys.

Service to God: Many of us have deep faith in a higher being and seek personal fulfillment in attaining the larger purpose in life. People are thought to be on earth for a reason, and finding and fulfilling our role in the divine plan is what most concerns us. God's intention for each of our lives can be very different—it is the fate of some to be successful in the world's view, and of others not to be. Personal fulfillment lies in understanding and accepting God's will for us in the faith that more important things lie beyond. Some of us have particular conceptions of God's design of our lives. Some believe that people are born incredibly selfish and are challenged in the rest of our lives to become completely selfless. This leads those of us who think this way to define success by the measure of the selflessness of our actions.

Service for the Good of Others: Some of us motivated by religious or humanistic convictions devote our lives to the service of others. We derive fulfillment from such a commitment. People in the helping professions such as health care and teaching are often especially motivated in this way. But service for the good of others is not limited to the helping professions. In business, it takes the form of steward or servant leadership in which executives seek to run the company for the good of investors, employees, customers and the community—who are said to be stakeholders of a firm.

Love: There are those of us who believe that ultimately love is the only thing in this world that is worth seeking. This leads us to judge our actions by the standard of whether or not they express love, and to receive love as the greatest of gifts.

Happiness. For many of us happiness is the very essence of personal fulfillment. We may define it as simply as this: when we wake in the morning, we are excited and interested in what our day has in store for us. We make our decisions on the basis of what will make us happy.

Building Character: For some of us life is a quest for personal growth. It is a personal journey toward building a strong character. The objective is to grow not what we have, nor what we do, but what we are. Personal tragedies and career setbacks, which we never seek but which happen anyway, are challenges that if we confront them properly add to our personal growth. The leadership we exercise is seen as a reflection of our personal development. Our ability to lead others is enhanced as we grow and our character deepens. By growing as a person we become more effective leaders and can help others grow. This view is furthest away from what is often offered us—a "recipe" for success, a list of strategies, skills, tactics—that we often instinctively look for from others.

These things are valuable in themselves, but are inevitably limited in value unless we can provide the personal growth that will make us acceptable to others because we bring something special to our leadership.

It should be apparent from the length of the list above and the significance of many of the items it includes that there is a significant personal element in the definition of fulfillment. It is very important that each of us think through what meaning fulfillment has for us. The danger of not doing so is that years from now we will say: "I have climbed the ladder of success, only to discover the ladder was leaning on the wrong wall."

That these many definitions of personal fulfillment often overlap dramatically is certain. Many of us would view a combination of several of these objectives as the measure of fulfillment in our lives.

Unfortunately, we don't necessarily understand what fulfills us. Some of us might think that if we get promoted to a top executive position in a big company before age forty, we will have attained success and happiness. Yet on reaching that goal, we may realize that we're unhappy because of the things we may have set aside in our single-minded pursuit of career advancement.

We probably will do better if we make our career, and personal, choices based not on financial rewards, but on a careful inquiry into what is going to bring us personal fulfillment. There is the danger that greed and ambition may drive us into lucrative but unfulfilling occupations that don't serve others and that don't provide personal growth. If so, then there's a danger in equating fulfillment or even happiness with money. In fact, it seems that most people adapt to income shifts up or down very quickly, which may mean that the lasting benefits of higher incomes after a moderate level is reached are essentially zero.

Problems with our definitions of personal fulfillment are not limited to career and money. For example, many of us turn to our families for all or much of our fulfillment in life, but family doesn't often work out—sadly, there are lots of divorces and bitter contests over divorce settlements. The result is that many people who seek fulfillment in their family lives experience deep disappointment.

Attitudes Toward Life

These observations about the dangers of placing too much of our hope for personal fulfillment in life in either career success or the affection of our families requires that we take note of one other question. Is personal fulfillment largely a result of how we view our world—that is, of our attitude toward life? Do most of us have in our lives enough to fulfill us, if only we recognized it? We can view each situation as a glass half-full or half-empty, focusing on what we have or what we have not.

We're all going to make mistakes in our futures—it is unavoidable—and if we react properly, we may be better people for our errors. But good attitudes toward life help yield success sometimes but happiness generally.

We should take an optimistic outlook—focusing on successes and opportunities, rather than on losses, failures and defeats. The more we undertake, and leaders take on very much, the more chance there is of failure, loss or defeat. But we can respond in ways that make ultimate achievement much greater.

EXECUTIVE SUMMARY 14-1

NINE WAYS OF VIEWING LIFE'S CHOICES

1. View a disappointment as an opportunity to learn—to profit from the experience—and recognize that this is the most important aspect of the disappointment.

2. Recognize that the significance of life is not in money and position, but in character building, in what we learn and what we become.

3. See that money is like oxygen, we and our organizations need it to survive. But life isn't about breathing. It's about what we do with our life.

4. Perceive that others don't love us for what we accomplish, but for what we are and how we treat them. When we treat them badly to advance our careers or increase our accomplishments, we earn not love but something very different.

5. Understand that our need for meaning in life isn't filled by what we get for ourselves, but by what we give to others. If there is a hole that we feel in our spiritual lives, then it isn't filled by money or position, but by what we give.

6. Devote time and effort to close relationships. Confiding and discussing problems and issues will help you resolve them.

Don't put these things aside for time spent on career advancement. At the end of our lives, we're unlikely to regret that we didn't spend more time at work.

7. Pause for reflection and meditate on the good things in life. Focusing on the good aspects of life helps prevent meaningless pursuit of pleasures simply as a diversion from setbacks and disappointments.

8. Practice being warm to others, having a sense of humor, adopting a positive outlook. These qualities will contribute both to our ability and acceptance as leaders and to our own sense of fulfillment in our lives.

9. Take pleasure in small things, even doing seemingly menial chores with energy and enthusiasm, because small differences in psychological perceptions can make a big difference in our attitudes toward life. In Chapter 2 we discussed fear as an obstacle to our becoming leaders—here is a way to overcome our fear, and it is as basic as our attitude toward life.

———————❖———————

In this book we've seen that leadership is not only charisma, it can be learned. Also, we've learned that what we do with our lives is a choice—and not a bad one; there are numerous options, and we can make the choice for ourselves.

However we find fulfillment in our lives, being an effective leader can make an important contribution. Learning the skills that make a leader successful and the ethical commitments that make leadership authentic, contributes to both the lives of those who benefit from our organizations, and also to our own lives. This is a very special thing about leadership.

Leadership: How to Lead, How to Live

ADDITIONAL READINGS:

Greenleaf, Robert K. **Servant Leadership, 25th Anniversary Edition.** Mahwah, N.J.: Paulist Press, 2002.

Kushner, Harold. **When Bad Things Happen to Good People.** New York: Schocken, 2001.

Niven, David. **The 100 Simple Secrets of Happy People: What Scientists Have Learned and How You Can Use It.** San Francisco: HarperSanFrancisco, 2000.

Spears, Larry C. **Insights on Leadership: Service, Stewardship, Spirit, and Servant-Leadership.** New York: John Wiley and Sons, Inc., 1998.

Leadership: How to Lead, How to Live

GLOSSARY

Accountability: The principle that those given responsibility or authority must account for one's actions and performance.

Active listening: Listening to what a speaker does and doesn't say; assessing the entire communication (including body language).

Administration: The development of plans and budgets, the staffing and operations of an organization.

Authority: The power or right to control, judge or prohibit the actions of others.

Charisma: Personal attractiveness and charm that enables influence over others.

Collegial leadership: A group of top executives or managers who consult and jointly make key decisions.

Commanding leadership style: A decisive approach to leadership; common in the United States.

Conflict resolution: A process of reaching agreement in a conflict situation.

Constructive criticism: The skill of giving criticism in way that helps resolve a problem and does not offend.

Corporate culture: The behavioral climate in an organization.

Demagogic leadership style: An emotional and manipulative approach to leadership based on stirring up emotional fervor.

331

Emotional resonance: The ability of a leader to mobilize the emotions of other people in driving towards certain goals.

Entrepreneurship: Starting and managing one's own business; the skills of those willing to risk their time and money in building a business.

Ethics: The inner compass that directs a person towards what is right and fair.

Expertise: Knowledge and skills that, employed by a leader, can help others do their jobs.

False leadership: Pretending to choose an organizational direction and direct and inspire.

Globalization: An increasing economic integration and interdependence across national borders.

Group think: Where group pressure damages the ability by decision-makers to make independent or moral judgments.

Hierarchy: Organizing or classifying according to rank or authority.

Servant leadership: An approach based on serving individuals and institutions first and leading from that motivation.

Staff management positions: Those managers who work in functions (such as personnel, strategic planning, logistics) supporting manufacturing and sales.

Strategy: A long-term plan to reach pre-defined goals.

Glossary

Leadership: A process by which one person influences the thoughts, attitudes and behaviors of others.

Line management position: Those managers involved in the production and sales of products and services.

Mentor: A senior person within a company or profession who counsels and guides a junior person's career. Some companies and organizations offer formal mentoring systems.

Mission: The guiding vision of an organization describing its goals and purpose.

Values: The set of beliefs we have about what is good and what is bad and how things should be.

Visionary leadership: Communicating the organization's vision and strategy in an inspirational way.

INDEX

A

Accountability, 232, 331
Active listening, 117, 331
Adaptability, 76, 77
Adelphia, 273
Administration, 17, 83, 331, 343
Advice, 198
Alcott, Louisa May, 215
Apple Computer, 85
Armstrong, Lance, 25
Arthur Andersen, 89, 90, 97, 224
Authority, 11, 15, 17, 20, 30, 32, 51, 63, 81, 246, 254, 331

B

Badaracco, Joseph L. Jr, 56
Balance
   work-life, 295
Belasco, James, 128, 137
Bell, Ella, 167
Bennis, Warren, 25, 27
Berkshire Hathaway, 53
Bolles, Richard Nelson, 243
Boyatzis, Richard, 79, 97
Brady, Diane, 49
Bstan-Dzin-Rgya-Mtsho, 67
Buffett, Warren, 53
Bush, George W., 35, 59, 60

C

Caesar, Vance, 213
Cappelli, Peter, 205
Career, 146, 315, 343
   balancing, 302
   choices, 156, 158
   exploring sweet spots, 162
   issues of not-for-profit jobs, 177

killers, 224
pitfalls, 216
shifts in, 163
sweet spots, 161
transition, 236
Career paths, 143
Caring, 58, 59
Caterpillar, 84
Charisma, 29, 60, 62, 331
   as basis for leadership, 49
Checklist
   for team leaders, 251
Churchill, Winston, 12, 317
Ciampa, Dan, 213
Citigroup, 273
Citrin, James M., 155, 167, 238, 243
Clinton, William J., 59, 60, 111
Collins, Jim, 97
Commanding leadership, 331
Commitment, 55, 60, 62, 184, 249
Communications, 111, 249
Confidence, 117
Conflict resolution, 249, 331
Conflicts of interest, 227
Constructive criticism, 252, 331
Conviction, 75, 76
Corporate culture, 331
Creative tension, 129
Cromwell, Oliver, 21

D

DBIO (Difference between income and outgo), 175
Decision making, 20, 248
Decisiveness, 74, 76, 235, 254, 256
DeGaulle, Charles, 51
Demagogic leadership, 93, 331
DePree, Max, 45
Digital Equipment Corporation (DEC), 105
Drucker, Peter F., 9, 343

E

Ellison, Larry, 186
Ellsworth, Richard R., 56, 67
Emotional resonance, 76, 78, 332

335

Emotional toughness, 76
Empathy, 60, 62, 79
Empowered teams, 256
Enron, 231, 273, 343
Entrepreneurship, 183, 332
Ethics, 229, 332
    definition of, 13
    importance of, 13
Excellent organization concept, 200
Expertise, 50, 60, 61, 254, 332

F

False leadership, 332
Family-friendly corporation, 305
Fiorina, Carly, 293
First Marblehead Corporation, 73
Fisher, Kimball, 263
Flattery
    dangers of, 234
Ford, Henry, 121
Fortune 100 companies, 205
Friedrich, Stephan A., 128
Friendship, 126, 127, 128
    in work-life balance, 310
Fuller, J.F.C., 22, 25

G

Gandhi, Mahatma, 265
Gandossy, Robert, 25
Gardner, John, 289
Garten, Jeffrey, 45
Gates, Bill, 105
General Electric Company (GE), 40, 87
George, Bill, 97
Gergen, David, 137
Gerstner, Louis, 137, 189
Globalization, 332
Goals, Empowerment, Measurement (GEM), 81
Goldsmith, Marshall, 128, 137
Goleman, Daniel, 79, 97
Gray, Loren, 208
Greenleaf, Robert K, 329
Group think, 332
Grove, Andrew S., 243

H

Hackman, J. Richard, 263
Hamon, Monika, 205
Harding, Warren, 49
Harley-Davidson, 22, 25
Harvard Business Review, 189, 206, 213, 224
Heifetz, Ronald A., 42, 45
Hewlett-Packard Corporation, 105, 293
Hierarchy, 332
Hinterhuber, Hans H., 128
Hitler, Adolf
    emotionalism of, 94
    evil leadership of, 13
    threat of, 12
Humility, 76, 80, 81

I

Integrity, 76, 77
Internal Revenue System, 23
International Business Machine Corporation (IBM), 86, 90, 105, 180, 181
Internet, 85, 105, 267, 280, 343

J

Jeanne D'Arc, 21
JetBlue, 109
Jobs, Steven, 85
Jones, Reginald, 94
Jordan, Michael
    brother of, 15
Julius Caesar, 35

K

Kabat-Zinn, Jon, 119
Katzenbach, Jon R., 122, 137, 263
Kellerman, Barbara, 226, 243
King, Martin Luther Jr., 21
Kotter, John P., 21, 25
Kubota, 84
Kushner, Harold, 329

L

L.L Bean, 194
Leadership, 25, 129, 165
   abilities in team setting, 258
   abilities of operational leader, 107
   and success, 55
   as role in life, 34
   as service, 81
   cooperative, 122
   definition of, 333
   empowering others, 88
   examples of, 22
   fear of, 42
   five central skills, 81
   five styles of, 92
   higher calling of, 19
   how it emerges, 32
   how it is crucial, 10
   in business, 22
   in government, 23
   in new economy, 271
   in relation to managing, administering, 17
   innate, bestowed or learned, 29
   meaning of, 11
   moral, 274
   moral, when attitudes shift, 279
   nature of, 20
   nine qualities of, 73
   operational, 102
   overcoming personal obstacles, 38
   personal fulfillment, 318, 320
   resisting evil, 210
   responsibility, 232
   styles in team setting, 256
   team, 254
   uses of, 13
   who gains from, 11
Lee, Robert E., 62, 232
Lichtenberg, Ronna, 243
Line positions, 178, 179, 333
   advantages of, 179
Linsky, Marty, 42, 45
Listening, 49, 113, 199, 251
   skills, 115, 259, 331

M

Maccoby, Michael, 213
Malraux, Andre, 51, 67
Management, 343, 344
   in old economy, 271
Mandela, Nelson, 67, 245
Marcus Aurelius, 233
Marketspace, 269
McGovern, Gail, 102, 103
McKee, Annie, 79, 97
Mentoring, 200, 333
   FAQs, 211
   formal, 201
Meyers, Dan, 73
Microsoft Corporation, 105
Mills, D. Quinn, 18, 25, 108, 119, 128, 136, 315, 343
Mintzberg, Henry, 99
Mission, 176, 333
Mother Teresa, 67
Mussolini, Benito, 94
Myths
   about work-life balance, 298
   division of labor, 299
   quality time, 300

N

Napoleon, 53, 54
National Aeronautics and Space Administration (NASA), 83, 84, 86
New Economy, 267
New York Stock Exchange, 73, 173
Niven, David, 329
Nkomo, Stella, 167
Not-for-profit organizations, 173, 174, 176, 177, 267

O

Octavian
   on leadership, 35
Olsen, Ken, 105
Oracle Corporation, 186
Organizations
   not-for-profit versus for profit, 173
   small versus large, 171
Ozley, Lee, 22, 25

P

Partnerships, 122, 124, 126, 129, 132, 133, 134
    disagreements, 135
    work-life balance, 312
Passion, 73, 74, 76
Personal fulfillment, 322
Pfeffer, Jeffrey, 39, 45, 97
Politics
    organizational, 206
Porras, Jerry, 97

R

Ready, Douglas A., 224
Reagan, Ronald W., 71, 111
Redmond, Andrea, 289
Reputation, 216
    at office, 219
Roosevelt, Eleanor, 47
Roosevelt, Franklin Delano, 40
    leadership skills, 40
Rossotti, Charles O., 23, 25

S

Search for excellence, 91
Segil, Larraine, 128, 137
Seifert, Dirk, 128
Self-awareness, 76, 80
Servant leadership, 332
Serven, Lawrence B. MacGregor, 119
Shalala, Donna, 53
Sheehy, Gail, 141
Smallwood, Norman, 82, 97
Smith, Richard A., 155, 167, 238, 243
Somerville, Ian, 136
Sonnenfeld, Jeffrey, 25
Spears, Larry C., 329
Staff positions, 178, 182, 332
Strategic myopia, 270
Strategy, 332
Success, 48, 53, 60, 62, 63, 79
    accepting recognition, 14
    keys for entrepreneur, 184
    ladder of, 324

of partnership, 126

T

Teams, 247
Teerlink, Rich, 22, 25
Thatcher, Margaret, 111, 169
Toffler, Barbara Lee, 90, 97, 224, 243
Tribbett, Charles A., III, 289
Trump, Donald, 109

U

Ulrich, David, 82, 97

V

Values, 56, 60, 62, 333
Vision, 83, 84, 85
Visionary leadership, 16, 333

W

Wal-Mart, 84
Washington, George, 61
Watkins, Michael, 189, 213
Welch, Jack, 40, 87, 94, 191
   leadership skills, 40
Whyte, David, 67
Work arounds, 208
WorldCom, 231, 273

Z

Zenger, Jack, 82, 97

Leadership: How to Lead, How to Live

About the Author

D. Quinn Mills is the Alfred J. Weatherhead Jr. Professor of Business Administration at Harvard Business School. He consults with major corporations and teaches at Harvard on subjects of leadership, strategy, and financial investments.

Mills had taught at MIT's Sloan School of Management between 1968 and 1975, and he supplemented his MIT teaching by spending several years in Washington, DC, assisting various government agencies. He is a Fellow of The National Academy of Human Resources and a member of the Panel of Thought Leaders of the Peter Drucker Foundation.

His books include: *Having It All ... and Making It Work: Six Steps for Putting Both Your Career and Your Family First*; *Wheel, Deal, and Steal: Deceptive Accounting, Deceitful CEOs and Ineffective Reforms*; and *Buy, Lie, and Sell High: How Investors Lost Out on Enron and the Internet Bubble*.

Dr. Mills earned his MA and Ph.D. from Harvard, both in economics, and received his undergraduate degree from Ohio Wesleyan University.

About MindEdge Press

The mission of MindEdge Press is to serve students and scholars by publishing books of the highest quality. Through its publishing activities, MindEdge Press seeks to promote the advance of scholarship and the development of knowledge.

MindEdge Press publishes books, white papers, teaching notes, and course materials focused on the areas of business and management, communications and effective writing, and online teaching methods and tactics.

MindEdge Press
1601 Trapelo Road
Waltham, MA 02451
www.mindedge.com